MINDBENDING

THE HUTCHISON FILES: 1981 TO 1995

George D. Hathaway, P. Eng.

Mindbending: The Hutchison Files: 1981 to 1995

Second Edition – 2016 – expanded edition with Publisher Notes

Integrity Research Institute Publishers
5020 Sunnyside Avenue, Suite 209
Beltsville MD 20705

www.IntegrityResearchInstitute.org
http://www.integrityresearchinstitute.org/catalog/mindbending.html

Cover design by Alicia Orlenko, Commercial Color Labs

Library and Archives Canada Cataloguing in Publication

Hathaway, George
Mindbending : the Hutchison files : 1981 to 1995 / George D. Hathaway.

Includes bibliographical references.

ISBN 978-1-935023-53-1

1. Hutchison, John, 1945-. 2. Parapsychologists--Canada--Biography. 3. Electromagnetic devices. 4. Antigravity. 5. Consciousness. I. Title.

BF1045.S33H38 2009
133.092
C2009-905920-7

First Edition – 2009 – published in Canada by
George D. Hathaway
1080 19th Sideroad
King City, Ontario
Canada, L7B 1K5

DEDICATION

This book is dedicated to the late Alex Pezarro who introduced me to John Hutchison, John Alexander who supported the early research in spite of its controversial nature and my father, Norman Hathaway, whose early interest made possible some of the investigations discussed in these pages.

ABOUT THE AUTHOR

George Hathaway is an electrical engineer with an abiding interest in the fringes of science. He owns and operates a research laboratory and has published many scientific and technical papers in peer-reviewed journals and books. In addition to lecturing on advanced energy and propulsion research, he has organized technical symposia and holds a US patent on a novel electrical machine. He lives with his wife in a forest north of Toronto.

Table of Contents

INTRODUCTION

We first called it the Lift and Disruption System and later the Hutchison Effect. The latter name stuck due to the impossibility of neatly categorizing just what was going on around John Hutchison in the years following 1980. And what was going on around John Hutchison was bizarre in the extreme. As with anything outside the realm of everyday experience, the Hutchison story eventually takes on mythical properties. It is a goal of this volume to reduce the mythological aspects of the early years of the Hutchison Effect and the man John Hutchison. This is not in any way meant to minimize the unbelievable nature of the manifestations attendant upon the Hutchison Effect, but merely to supply history with an account of this fascinating man and his accomplishments. This book is intended for the reader interested in following the historical development from correspondence as it happened as well as the more technically-oriented reader interested in gaining a deeper perspective on how the phenomena might have been made manifest.

What is the Hutchison Effect? It is a collection of phenomena lying far outside our normal experience and understanding. Its primary manifestations include causing or allowing objects of any material to lift into the air either in a vertical or looping trajectory or to hover; severely disrupting intermolecular bonds in any material resulting in catastrophic disruptive fracturing; causing plastic deformation in metals; creating unusual aurora-like lighting effects in mid-air; and inducing changes in the magnetic state and chemical composition of metals. All these effects were produced on test samples placed on a rough wooden table where the closest piece of John's apparatus was several feet away. No connections were made to the samples whatsoever and the entire apparatus operated from one or two household electrical outlets.

Currently there is a plethora of sources offering information and commentaries about the Hutchison Effect[1]. In the early 1980s when various symposia and conferences on "free energy" along with the work of Nikola Tesla[2] were an almost yearly occurrence, the Hutchison Effect was introduced. I mentioned it during one of my lectures on proper measurement techniques at the 1983 Second International Symposium on Non-Conventional Energy Technology in Atlanta, GA. The first full public disclosure giving technical details and results of engineering measurements was given by me at the 1988 New Energy Technology Symposium in Hull, Quebec, organized by the Planetary Association for Clean Energy, Ottawa, Canada.[3] Thereafter, articles appeared in numerous venues. Now a Google search of "Hutchison Effect" on the internet reveals about 4,490,000 hits (as of 03/09).

My involvement in the Hutchison Effect started in 1980 through my late friend Alexis Pezarro of Vancouver, BC, Canada. I had come to know Alex after inquiring into the activities of the Planetary Association for Clean Energy (PACE). This organization was one of the first groups to investigate the area of "Emerging Science" as it came to be known. It is still active and investigates and reports on areas usually sidelined by mainstream journalism such as parapsychology, alternative medicine, and non-conventional

---

[1] For a different historical perspective, see Manning, J. "Rainbow in the Lab: The John Hutchison Story", Amber Bridge Books, Vancouver, BC, 1992

[2] Pub. Note: For our younger readers, Nikola Tesla gave us AC electricity, in spite of the vehement, legal opposition from Thomas Edison. Read any of the biographies of Nikola Tesla to appreciate why he became an underground hero or simply watch the two minute rap video which tells the annotated full history: http://www.epicrapbattlesofhistory.com/video/xegNhFa6IAda/search/edison

[3] Pub. Note: Dr. Andrew Michrowski, Planetary Association for Clean Energy (PACE), 1001 Bronson Avenue, #1001, Ottawa, Ontario K1R6G8, Canada

energy and propulsion technologies, amongst others. Its director, Dr. Andrew Michrowski, put me in touch with Alex who was looking for an engineer to help him understand an interesting electronic device he was using to locate hydrocarbon deposits. Shortly after contacting Alex in Vancouver and discussing the hydrocarbon device, he told me about his encounter with a most fascinating man, John Hutchison.

As Alex related, he was visiting a psychic fair in Vancouver sometime in 1979 or 1980 and came across the booth of a Mr. Mel Winfield. Mel was demonstrating various pieces of high voltage apparatus, including a Tesla coil, to attract attention to his booth. Apparently, Mel's main purpose for the booth was to promote his new theory unifying gravity and electromagnetism. On the table he had arrayed a selection of Polaroid photographs. These showed various articles such as a rifle, sabre saw, rings of copper pipe and other items floating in mid-air above a cloth-draped background. Alex was naturally intrigued and asked Mel how he got the articles to defy gravity long enough to be photographed. Mel stated that it was a combination of electrostatic and electromagnetic fields which were configured according to his new electromagnetic theory of gravity. He further said that he had contracted a machinist to help repair a van de Graaff electrostatic machine which was essential for the operation of the invention. In late summer of 1981, Mel at last showed Alex where the apparatus was operating, namely in John's basement lab in Lynn Valley, BC. This was the "machinist" who had repaired the van de Graaff machine. Alex's interest was further piqued when he found pieces of shattered metal in the garbage can in the lab. John's apparatus had been fracturing large metal bars of aluminum and steel by mistake and John was throwing them out, complaining "'I can't machine these, they're useless now!'"

Alex knew that I was organizing and hosting the First International Symposium on Non-Conventional Energy at the University of Toronto in October 1981 and suggested that we have Mel make a presentation on this work. Although we considered having both John and Mel give a joint presentation in Toronto, John suffered from acute agoraphobia and avoided all open spaces as much as possible. So Alex and I paid for Mel's trip and accommodation only to find out later that the actual discoverer of the phenomenon was John Hutchison.

At various times John has told different stories about how he discovered the lifting phenomenon. One is that he learned of the effect while experimenting in the dark and noticing things had moved when the lights were turned back on. Another time he explained to me that a phenolic block flew into the air and hit him on the shoulder while working with the apparatus. Yet a third explanation was that a 1.25" thick bakelite block tipped over in the lab while he was watching.

George Hathaway

King City, Ontario

2009

PART I: In His Own Words

I am fortunate that John was a conscientious letter writer. I insisted that even if he didn't keep detailed lab notes, his numerous letters and faxes would prove very useful in the future. It is from this hand-written correspondence that the narrative of his life and my involvement in it is reconstructed. The best way to get a flavour of the man is through his letters and I quote them at some length. Most of the letters are dated which allows the roughly chronological sequence of events to be set down. Where necessary I have paraphrased and corrected spelling and grammar to be more readable without altering the sense. [My editorial comments are in square brackets.]

This volume ends in 1995. There are several reasons for this. After that year, our correspondence became much more limited as John pursued other directions for the Hutchison Effect. As I wish to use his own words wherever possible, continuation past 1995 would greatly diminish the impact of the presentation. In addition, my friend Alex Pezarro's untimely death silenced this trusted independent information channel to John's activities. My consulting business was heading in new directions and my involvement with John on a more-or-less continual basis had gradually ceased. Finally, as John pursued the media and they pursued him, the Hutchison Effect phenomena as I knew it effectively stopped in the early 1990s. John began emphasizing his home-made energy generators. Although there has been a flurry of recent videotapes for TV shows, as I have not been personally or indirectly involved, I cannot comment with any certainty after the mid-1990s.

1981: John, Alex Pezarro & Mel Winfield

The earliest correspondence from John consists of hand-written technical notes from September, 1981 to me. In what was to become typical fashion, John is very curt when describing technical details of the experiment. The following is the earliest written description of the Hutchison apparatus:

- standing columnar waves [after Tesla]
- rapid decay 4-7cps [waveshape and repetition rate in cycles per second, now called Hertz or Hz]
- mass distribution [of masses in the vicinity of the effect]
- watch for bright spot on centre of [main] Tesla coil
- spark gap does not arc but [fuzzy] discharges [are seen on] on terminals [of spark-gap capacitor]
- 200-400 kHz, wattage 1000 [small radio transmitter]
- radioactive material – thorium [later uranium ore] – put into copper tube 2" x 15", with 3 vacuum tubes surrounding [it]
- suppress sparks [from top of main Tesla coil]
- 15, 30, 60 kV [various high voltage transformers]
- ½ second discharge of van de Graaff via spark gap and capacitor

Here, John is outlining the essential system components of the earliest version of his apparatus. More detailed descriptions are presented in the technical section, Part II.

In October, 1981, the First International Symposium on Non-Conventional Energy was held at the University of Toronto, Canada. Thanks to the good offices of Prof. Charles Hanly of the Department of Philosophy, I was able to organize and host the symposium at University College and about 150 people from around the world attended. The theme of the symposium echoed that of a similar conference[4] held in 1980 in Hannover, Germany, hosted by the late oncologist Dr. Hans Nieper. Both conferences were dedicated to finding new energy and propulsion theories and technologies which were beginning to be developed far from the mainstream of science.

Presentations ranged from extracting useful work from differences in gravitational potential, to more efficient acoustically-cataysed water hydrolysis, to new force production methods and methods of interacting with and modifying the local gravitational field[5].

Alex Pezarro had arranged for Mel Winfield to make a technical presentation on the work of John Hutchison as my prime interest in organizing the symposium was to show actual working hardware. In the belief that Mel was the developer of the hardware that produced the bizarre effects, we hoped to learn about how the effects were created. Unfortunately, Mel was only interested in furthering his own theories, which had no correspondence with the reality of the Hutchison Effect. Mel's description of the Hutchison Effect was limited to a few minutes at the end of his talk and only in the context of using it

---

[4] Pub. Note: Gravity Field Energy Conference, Nov., 1980, summarized in *Dr. Nieper's Revolution in Technology, Medicine, and Science*, MIT Verlag, 1985

[5] Proceedings of this and the Second International Symposium on Non-Conventional Energy which I co-hosted in Atlanta, GA. are available from the Planetary Association for Clean Energy, Ottawa, Canada.

as a proof of the veracity of his theories. We were most disappointed.

During the latter part of 1981 many effects were personally witnessed by Alex and, apparently, members of the Murphy family in whose basement John had established his 'laboratory'. John lived in the basement and slept on a cot alongside his equipment. He lived very simply, with virtually all his income from a government disability pension he received due to his agoraphobia. This condition necessitated his taking several psychoactive drugs which kept the condition somewhat under control. He disliked having to rely on them and was greatly relieved when, a decade later, he was able to reduce his reliance on them. As we shall see, however, this also coincided with the inability to reproduce the original effects which made him famous.

John was a self-taught experimenter whose great love was constructing high-frequency and high-voltage apparatus invented in the late 1900s by the Serbian-American electrical genius Nikola Tesla. In particular, he wished to duplicate Tesla's attempts to transmit electrical power using radio waves. In fact, it was this type of experimentation that, he claimed, led to the accidental discovery of the Hutchison Effect. Much of his day was spent rummaging through surplus electronics stores and junk yards in search of pieces of military electronics to try to make operational again, sometimes for use in his ever-changing apparatus. He was constantly turning metal pieces on his lathe and machining various pieces of metal for inclusion in his electrical experiments.

Tesla coils fascinated John from an early age. He made many varieties, from rotary spark gap types to fixed gaps to vacuum tube oscillator types. Often these were shown at science fairs. Evidently John met Mel at one of these fairs in the late 1970s. Another love of his was collecting small arms such as military rifles and pistols plus the odd small cannon. He had amassed a small collection before Alex and I met him but had most of it confiscated by police in 1967-68. He was in the midst of a court struggle to have the pieces returned when Alex met him.

He had only one very close friend, Bill Ross. “Billie” was his confidante and sometime assistant and seemed to be involved in all aspects of John's personal life. Billie helped John through the various crises that would afflict him from time to time. In a letter from early 1981, John writes: “...we are like brothers...He pushed me out of my agoraphobic condition.” Unfortunately, John’s assessment of his condition was premature. As the years went by, John started to become known internationally. This brought him into contact with women for the first time and serious relationships ensued. Billie and John eventually separated.

1982: The Famous 8mm Movies; Pharos Tech

In 1982 John was still living in the Murphy's basement at 1458 E 29th, Lynn Valley, BC. Alex and I had offered to get John to Toronto to help me set up a new laboratory for experiments with John but he declined due to problems with his current landlord. In a letter to me from March 9, he says our offer is a 'Golden Opportunity' but one that he will have to pass up.

Important insights into his early abilities are found in letters from 1982;

> Since I was 5 years old, I could "feel" things. Yes I know it sounds rather crazy …but I know and feel and understand what I am building.
>
> I have visions of … machines to build: – I see them, I feel them. I must with my machine tools build them. I must do it with a maddening FEVER, A PASSION [emphasis JH]. I have been like this always.
>
> I study and feel electromagnetic energy.

By this time, he had already demonstrated lifting many objects to Mel Winfield and wanted to demonstrate the effects to my father, Norman Hathaway, myself and Alex Pezarro. He emphasized soaking all electrical parts in varnish and transformer oil to prevent unwanted electrical arcing due to the high voltages produced by parts of his apparatus.

As the year went on, John became concerned about Mel's behaviour, especially towards Alex. Mel realized that Alex and I represented a threat to his ideas about gravity as we tried to convince John to allow reputable scientists to examine his apparatus. To our great satisfaction, John was very keen to involve scientists and engineers in trying to determine how the effects were produced and how to improve reliability. John was the first to admit that he did not understand exactly how the apparatus affected objects. At this point, Mel was trying to raise funds to further his own theories and experiments based on John's discoveries. Mel considered John's work a vindication of his theory of gravity and was interested in promoting it more than understanding it. John admitted: "He is getting mixed up with some kind of strange people" referring to Mel's quest for funding. In February, I visited John and Alex in Vancouver and we met Mel who was living above his Universology Book Store on Davie St., an early 'new-age' store specializing in crystal healing, fringe science, etc. I was not impressed by Mel's theories.

Alex had provided John with an 8mm movie film camera, alas with no sound. In March, John had taken the first films of the phenomenon. This included hanging "rainbow" luminescence, metal melting without apparent heat, objects wobbling back and forth or hovering and suddenly taking off and strange magnetic effects. These films constitute the most important record of the first phase of the operation of the apparatus.

In the same month, he described the heart of the system in his own words:

> The heart of the system is Tesla's but uses a "shaped" [field] generator. It has a [hollow] steel ball on top with rings. From here the various

> "bits" of electrical impulses... feed the chokes, capacitors, variometers and metal bars. [The radio frequency generator] is 400 kHz CW variable pulse [width] 500 watts damped field. Also sonics: I use sometimes 10-30000 cps to vibrate "loose" coils. The van de Graaff pulse on a scope would look like [damped oscillation] decay pulse. It bunches 5 to 20 per second.

John's concerns about Mel were growing. "Mel just writes books taking everyone for a ride and never gets anywhere. Takes Tesla and turns all Tesla's work into his own...Mel has a [channeled] guide from outer space or Atlantis." In his search for funds to continue his research into gravity, Mel introduced John to "a reckless lying man (Calvin) - high promoter – insulted my intelligence and my machines. He could offer me $5 million, I would have gladly thrown it back at him" to quote John. Here John gets a preview of what will plague him the rest of his life, namely people who wish to appropriate his discoveries or make money promoting them: "I must watch these characters..."

Alex was also growing concerned about Mel's agenda and how it was affecting John's experimentation. John was trying to understand the deals that Mel and others were offering but lamented his lack of business sense "Good grief, I am ignorant of business". He seemed much more comfortable dealing with Alex who he described as "...one hell of a guy – so full of life and vigour and understanding. I feel so at ease with him."

In April, Alex and I, together with my father, formed Pharos Technologies Inc., registered in Vancouver, BC. Eventually, Pharos came to be the negotiating instrument for raising funds for several attempted demonstrations of the Hutchison Device as well as promoting the understanding and use of the hydrocarbon detector.

Alex had acquired the rights to the hydrocarbon detection device some years prior from someone in Florida who said they obtained it from a radio engineer in England. As the device was based on vacuum tubes, it required a large and heavy battery pack to be carried into the field with it. Alex later engaged the services of two men, Alexander Shereshevsky and George Liszicasz, who claimed that they were engineers and could transistorize the device for Alex to make it lighter, and also apply micro-computer technology to enhance the output presentation. Evidently, they were not able to do what they had claimed and in the process, effectively destroyed the original device. Alex's initial interest in me was to see if I could reproduce the original device in tube form from some of the circuit diagrams that Alex had kept. This I was able to do to Alex's satisfaction, but I never did ascertain exactly the principle on which the device worked.

We will hear more from Shereshevsky and Liszicasz later in the story. Incidentally, both men went on to claim that they had independently invented hydrocarbon detectors and formed many companies trying to promote the use of the device. Shereshevsky apparently gave up in the 1990s but Liszicasz is now the CEO of a large Canadian oil and gas exploration company, NXT Energy Solutions Inc. The description of the exploration technology, which Liszicasz claims to have invented but is impossible to patent for "proprietary reasons" is remarkably similar to that used by Alex Pezarro in the 1980s.

From the time I met John until the mid-1980s, Pharos tried with varying degrees of success to raise money to further John's experiments. During 1982, several potential financiers were canvassed including Dr. Morgan Raiford of Atlanta, tobacco heir Josh Reynolds, inventor Alexis Guy Obolensky, the mysterious Dr. Brana of San Diego and entrepreneur James Black who had supported a novel propulsion device invented by Robert Cook.

By July 1982, we were trying to finance John's move to another, more secure location and pay him a salary. He wanted to find a place where he could be left alone for long periods of time so as to concentrate on his apparatus. John had been tinkering with some of his own "free energy" device ideas, including crystals and permanent magnets.

Meanwhile I was sending John some needed apparatus and materials to assist in his experimentation. He noted that the Murphy house had been hit by lightning three times with damage to the home and neighbour's home but fortunately no damage to John's basement lab. John complained of "microwave clicks" in his ears, which he said were common for radar technicians working with high-powered microwave transmitters. He telephoned his doctor, Murray Allen, who told him to "lay off the high frequency fields", advice John thankfully ignored.

Alex was also keen in having John examine some well-known "free energy" devices to see if John's unique abilities could enable them to work. Alex and I had recently visited Robert Alexander in the USA and brought back a rotating machine purportedly able to produce excess energy. John started experimenting with it but eventually gave up in frustration. It never preformed as claimed, but it solidified John's fascination with energy-producing devices.

Prior to May, I had discussed John's work with Tom Valone who lived at that time in Buffalo, NY and was an instructor at a local college. I had met Tom at Dr. Nieper's Hannover symposium along with many other fascinating individuals who would all have their influence on the underground "free energy" movement. These included Adam Trombly who, along with Bruce DePalma, was experimenting with coupled Faraday homopolar disk generators[6], John Searl who was becoming legendary for his claims of building an anti-gravity craft in his backyard in Britain several years before, Rolf Schaffranke, the author of a seminal pamphlet on the levitation experiments of Thomas T. Brown[7] amongst others,

---

[6] Pub. Note: See *The Homopolar Handbook: A Definitive Guide to Faraday Disk and N-Machine Technologies* by Thomas Valone, Integrity Research Institute Publishers, 1994, available on Amazon.com, for stories about DePalma and Trombly who developed their homopolar generators at the same time as Valone.

[7] Pub. Note: Ether-Technology: A Rational Approach to Gravity Control by Rolf Schaffranke (using the pseudonym "Rho Sigma") is still a 'pamphlet' size and available on Amazon.com. It was the inspiration for the two Electrogravitics books

Rudolf Zinsser who had invented a force-producing machine based on electrical pulses in water, and several others. Tom himself was completing a Faraday disk machine[8] at the time and we discussed the Hutchison Effect with Tom's electrical engineering professor at the State University of New York, Prof. Richard Dollinger. Dollinger was intrigued but suggested a list of possible prosaic methods for providing lift, including vibrating tables, electrostatic lift, electric field gradients, magnetic levitation, piezoelectric effects, etc. All of these were certainly possible but on a scale of activity far smaller than that occurring in the Hutchison apparatus. Incidentally, Dollinger suggested to us that the Ark of the Covenant might have been a dry battery. Interestingly John was asked to make a replica of the Ark twenty years later for a television program.

In Toronto, I had been busy constructing an electromagnetically shielded room in my small laboratory in Toronto for Hutchison experiments. In a May 25 letter from Lynn Valley, John congratulated me on assembling the equipment and lab space after I sent him some photographs. He needed transformer laminations and other equipment which I supplied. Alex and I were still trying to coax John into coming to Toronto to assist the lab set up but John said he wanted to get the Alexander machine tests out of the way. The real reason for his reticence was his agoraphobia as well as leaving his mate, Bill Ross. If he came, he says, he would want to bring Bill Ross as he "is a great help to me".

John also stated that he had all the parts to make a Moray device and would point out to us what Moray did to get his device working. This device, developed by Henry Moray of Salt Lake City in the 1930s, is the archetypical example of "free energy" devices. It is claimed to have produced up to 5000 watts of high-frequency power using only energy drawn from a long-wire antenna and a good earth ground. In some

---

about T.T. Brown mentioned in the next footnote. Volume I also includes the only T.T. Brown diagram of his circuit, reprinted from Rho Sigma's booklet.

[8] Pub. Note: *The Zinsser Effect* book, *Electrogravitics* Vol. I & II, which George refers to, all edited by Tom Valone, Integrity Research Institute Publishers, available from Amazon.com

tests, apparently even the earth ground was not required, as in the tests on board aircraft. Alex was slowly introducing John to more interesting energy devices in the hopes that, while John was not working on his own experiments, he might be able to shed some light on these other intriguing devices. I sent John information on several "free-energy" devices, notably the German Hans Coler[9] and American Hendershot permanent magnet systems, as well as the "N-Machine" of Bruce DePalma. Alex also provided John a sample of a mineral called a "Yuma Stone" which Alex purchased while attending a conference in California on psychotronics, the study of mind-matter interaction. This sample of rock was supposed to generate a small amount of electricity when electrodes were attached to the surface. Alex and I could never see this effect and, naturally, Alex wanted to see if John was able to detect or stimulate any current. John failed, but it started him thinking about generating electricity from minerals and resulted eventually in the production of his "Dirt-Cheap" or "Shake and Bake" energy cells in the late 1990s. Incidentally, T. T. Brown, mentioned above, was also interested in a similar investigation which he called petro-electricity.[10]

At this point also, Alex introduced John to the "scalar wave" ideas of Col. Thomas Bearden.[11] Tom Bearden was a speaker at the First International Symposium on Non-Conventional Energy where he discussed his ideas about how the Russians were preparing and testing advanced electromagnetic weapons to be used against the West based on something he called Tesla scalar-wave technology. Tom's theory was that

---

[9] Pub. Note: "The Invention of Hans Coler, Relating to an Alleged New Source of Power" by R. Hurst, British Intelligence Objectives Committee, 1946, is reprinted by Integrity Research Institute, supplemented with related articles on the Coler device.

[10] Pub. Note: See the twelve minute segment in the two hour video online called "Free Energy: Race to Zero Point" where John shows and explains petro-electricity, as well as the lift and disruption of metal objects.

[11] Pub. Note: Visit http://www.cheniere.org/ which is called "The Tom Bearden Website" to learn about Bearden's theories, videos, books, and more. He has been a coauthor of peer-reviewed journal articles on scalars, energy from the vacuum, and more.

Tesla had discovered a novel type of electromagnetic radiation which was longitudinal in nature, like sound waves, unlike the usual (transverse) radio waves. Tesla alluded to similar phenomena which he termed “columnar standing waves”. Tom called them scalar waves. I had presented John’s research results to Tom Bearden after the symposium, and he immediately used scalar waves to explain John’s various phenomena. John and Tom corresponded frequently and John became quite taken by Tom’s theories, so much so that John sometimes referred to his apparatus as a “Scalar Wave Generator”

In the same May 25 letter, John discussed the apparatus and describes more effects taking place, some with Alex as witness:

> Alex viewed the Scalar Wave Generator. We had extreme angular [sloping] lift. The night previous I had 6 inch lift... I hope Alex can lend me a camera again... more horizontal control as Alex viewed a 30 degree [lift ending in a] sharp drop off at 2 feet.
>
> I started years ago my first experiments with electromagnetic energy, corona and vibration. At that time I was using mass in a blanket of electromagnetism. Any mass introduced would cause a shift in frequency of the RF [radio frequency] picked up on radio receiver. My first attempts were to use a large toroid on the floor plus 30 kV DC 5 microAmp flyback horizontal output stage [transformer] similar to a TV set to cause static – plastic, paper and glass only would ‘fly around’... I [use] my lathe to build certain focusing units to direct this energy on any object.
>
> I had a 2 inch piece of steel turn black at one end ... some layers of this piece turned to fine

airborne dust… dents and pin-holes in it [shown in Fig. 9 in Part III].

John went on to describe a small radioactive source in a copper tube which was sometimes connected to the plates of a new double triode oscillator Tesla coil he was now using in place of the 400 kHz generator. He later mentioned how humidity and geomagnetic storms influenced the effects. He reported on a leaking capacitor and a shorted 30 kilovolt (kV) transformer and requested I send him information on "Pyranol", the oil apparently filling it. Pyranol is a common PCB-based electrical insulating oil. Unfortunately, many of John's capacitors and transformers contained Pyranol as he had retrieved them from scrap dealers. I cautioned John about the problems he would face if he didn't get rid of these devices. In fact, just this problem was to become a major reason why John lost much of his laboratory a decade later. He describes the transformer problem:

> I built a mid-tuned double toroidal Tesla transformer [a horizontal Tesla coil with two large electrodes at opposite ends – see, for example Fig. 18] suspended from the ceiling. [There was a] powerful flash in the basement then the 30 kV unit went dead. Lighted up the back yard like a photoflash.

John lamented his tardiness at producing a working Alexander device:

> This is why perhaps Alex's Alexander device is so slow to come into reality: I don't crave it. Please understand this odd thing about me. This is why I could never hold down a 9 to 5 "common job" but an 8 AM to 1 AM sometimes 24 hour

> job... The greatest thing is all the knowledge to learn in such a short time.

In Vancouver John was getting effects sometimes on demand and sometimes only one effect in 2-4 days. Typical of his descriptions:

> While at 2 AM ...with some test samples on the board... what I saw was almost a sense of unreality – these samples looked alive as they distorted... Woke up old man Murphy.

John wrote to me that "to fully equip the Toronto lab", I will need:

- [transformer] lamination stock
- Cloth covered wire #30, 36, 18, 20, 12
- Variable capacitors – 13 to 20 kV
- Copper spheres 6" to 18"
- Aluminum capacitor, loose fit, foil wound inside a plastic pail
- Spark gap, air blown or electromagnet[ically blown]
- Insulator stock
- Winding frame for coils
- Larger [electro-]static machine 500,000 to 1,000,000 volts
- Standing wave chokes [?].

I had already set about trying to obtain as many of the necessary items as possible.

After much prodding, John finally agreed to fly to Toronto in July to advise me on aspects of the lab I had started and meet with those interested in his work, including my father, James Black and several others. The trip was harrowing for John as he had to expend much effort to keep his agoraphobia under control. This included hiding under a blanket with the window shades drawn on the airplane and cringing inside the back seat of our car in Toronto. He was particularly concerned about the correct placement of the larger objects in my lab such as high-voltage transformers and capacitors, as well as the electrostatic machines. As it turned out, I never did amass enough equipment in that lab to attempt a replication along the lines that John had originally specified. As we learned more about John's capabilities and proclivities, it began to be clear that we would be wasting our time equipping an independent lab if John himself was not present the whole time.

James Black was Canadian but had moved to California and had in the late 1970s become interested in "free energy" and advanced propulsion technology in association with his church. Having raised money therefrom to support inventor Robert Cook,[12] he was naturally intrigued with John's work which I told him about during the 1981 symposium in Toronto. Black had fallen out with Cook by mid-1982 and had found another inventor of an even "better" propulsion system involving rotating depleted uranium masses invented by Anthony Taves. My father agreed to let Taves have a space in his office building in downtown Toronto if Black paid the rent, Taves' fees, etc. During this time we were negotiating with Black to help fund the Hutchison work. Black never did end up supporting John's work, although we had arrived at the stage of having a contract prepared but never signed. Several months later we learned that Black had run out of money and was not able to support either Taves or John. Taves was desperate to learn the "secret" of John's machine. This he

---

[12] Pub. Note: Robert Cook presented his unique inertial propulsion invention slideshow at the First Symposium on Non-Conventional Energy Technology. His book *The Death of Rocketry*, has been updated and edited by his son, Robert Cook, Jr. and is available on Google Books and Lulu.com.

never did, but wrote a report on how he thought it may function based on general information I had supplied him. A year and a half later, after running up many unpaid bills and operating on my father's largesse, it was time to say goodbye to Tony Taves.

By August, the Toronto office of Pharos Technologies Inc was in my father's Toronto office. I was supplying John with voltmeters, ammeters, wattmeters and machine tools. We had termed John's device LID – the Lift Induction Device and later LADS – the Lift And Disruption System. John mentioned that the Murphys were going to sell their house in January 1983 so Pharos had to start seriously considering moving John out of the Murphy's basement. This was to be a great concern to John as he had amassed such a large quantity of equipment and guns. But John was committed to working with Pharos with whom, after considerable deliberation, he had signed a working agreement:

> I would be happy to [continue to] work with your group [i.e. Pharos]. There is no way in my power will I see Pharos go under. Alex, your patience is incredible... your kindness will always be remembered.

This first Pharos agreement bound John as a consultant to be paid professional fees in accordance with an agreed-to schedule of demonstrations, the purpose of which was to raise the capital needed to set up John in a proper laboratory where the effect could be scientifically studied. John was living day to day from his disability pension which stipulated that if he found a job (i.e. became employed), he would lose his benefits. John was very concerned about that potential loss due to a failure of Pharos or a bad demonstration or other problem. The consulting arrangement, whereby John was not considered an employee, was deemed the best solution for moving forward. By October, John had suggested a few amendments to the Pharos contract with regard to royalties, responsibilities, etc.

He was concerned that Pharos not take legal action in the event that the machine destroyed itself or did not work properly. He was also advised by his father, Kenneth G. Hutchison, against letting go of control of the technology if a working unit was set up in Toronto. It was typical of John to sign a contract after careful consideration and discussion only to be swayed by others later into adding this or that clause, or even quitting the contract altogether. Knowing John's vicissitudes, Alex advised that we treat contracts with John more lightly than with other people if we wanted to continue good working relations with him. Thus we never took legal action when John broke his contracts with us.

John was always interested in obtaining more high-voltage power supplies. I had met Filippo Galluppi through the First International Symposium and had told him about John's apparatus. He was the founder of Venus Scientific in Farmingdale, New York, a company which supplied high-voltage power supplies to many industries, but now part of Eldec Corp. We also were hoping that he might be inclined to invest in the technology with more than a transformer or two. I had come to Vancouver in November in hopes of witnessing an "event" for myself since Alex had informed me that the apparatus was operating well. Filippo also came with his wife, Mary, and together we witnessed and I filmed a remarkable metal fracturing event. This was a 4 inch long steel bushing about 2 inches in outer diameter with a 1 inch hole through it (see Fig. 8). It was placed by me into the "active area" and within several minutes of John's tuning, a large piece just fractured off the end with a slight "crack". Later I myself witnessed the levitation of a small ferrite piece. Filippo was intrigued but was not able to assist in the financing of further explorations into the Hutchison Effect. He did, however, loan John a 1 kVA 30 kV high-voltage power supply that John needed.

Prior to this demonstration to Filippo, Mary, Alex and myself, John had been showing the effects to many other people including Mel Winfield, Mel's son, members of the

Murphy family, especially one son, Mark Murphy, Alex, Bill Ross plus many gun collector friends of John's.

During my time at John's first laboratory in the Murphy's basement, I made detailed measurements of all the equipment that, according to John, was important to obtaining the effects. This included complete circuit diagrams, some of which are included in Part II of this book.

Late in 1982, the first of many demonstrations that didn't work was given to people sent to witness the effect by Dr. Brana of San Diego, through whom we were attempting to obtain financial support for John. According to John, Brana's men were very condescending and mocked the apparently haphazard assortment of equipment that represented John's life's work. In a foul mood, John gave a half-hearted demonstration which did not impress the visitors. "They wrote it off to springs and electromagnets" John wrote in reference to their explanation of the events they had been shown on film previously by Alex and myself. That demonstration was to have been worth $250,000.

1983: The INSCOM/US Army Demonstration

The year started with a letter to me in reference to the Toronto laboratory containing:

> Very important notes to George: tank circuit important – Tesla would call this the extra coil. A constant phase will suspend object for longer periods. Keep sparks down to a fuzz between gaps. Your earth is very important – you may need to vary your earth. Primary [of large Tesla coil] should always be 10,000 to 100,000 volts AC 60 Hz. [Note: circuit diagrams drawn from working apparatus at the time show no direct connections to primary from any high-voltage power supply.]

John also thanked Filippo for the loan of the power supply and mentioned he was interested in working on Alex's oil and gas detector. He was starting to expand his interests as he stated his desire to investigate:

- Earthquake prediction
- Ball electricity
- Free energy

- Energy amplification
- Time variance
- Lift devices
- Metal transformation
- Beam electronics
- New age physics

Lamenting his poor demonstration for the San Diego group and the resulting concerns that Alex and I had about finding the best method of working with John in a structured business environment, John stated:

> Alex is on his diet. I've never met such a dynamic person. I know I have strained your and Alex's friendship… Alex pointed out I am my own worst enemy – This is true… I know this Pharos enterprise is my only chance.
>
> I did so much at Christmas '82. I wish you [GDH] were around… I had so much fun, powerful feelings into these experiments…[I] know what to do exactly to cause effects, happiness was with me and freedom."

John found out in January that the Murphy's had sold the house and John would have to move out by the end of March. We had to move quickly if we were to secure John in a proper location.

In January, Alex had been discussing possible NASA purhad invited to speak at the first symposium. Although this was not forthcoming, interest was shown by the US Army via Col. John Alexander[13] through a unit with the acronym

---

[13] Pub. Note: Col. Alexander also headed the Human Factors department for the US Army. His biography is online: http://www.johnbalexander.com/biography

INSCOM (Intelligence and Security Command). Alex had met Col. John Alexander at a recent psychotronics conference[14] in the US. INSCOM was headed at that time by Maj. Gen. Bert Stubblebine who was in the midst of several unusual and exotic programs for enhancing the Army's strategic and tactical capabilities by investigation of parapsychological areas such as telekinesis and remote viewing. A similar investigation had been underway at SRI International under the direction of Dr. Harold "Hal" Puthoff[15] that included training of INSCOM personnel in such capabilities. Dr. Puthoff was to figure later in the Hutchison saga.

Alex and I had arranged a preliminary meeting in Arlington, VA to discuss the possibility of INSCOM assistance in understanding the Hutchison Effect in February. It had never been our intention to develop the Hutchison Effect into an offensive weapon. But we knew that if we did not go to the military, they would come to us sooner rather than later. So we collectively decided that it would be prudent to present John's work to a branch of a friendly military that would be at least somewhat open to the possibilities.

We briefed Maj. Gen. Stubblebine who became very interested after John Alexander showed him a rod of molybdenum apparently used in a nuclear reactor which he had sent to Alex and which John had recently bent up. Alex had taken the rod plus other samples sent by Col. Alexander and placed them in the "active area" and while watching the rod bend back and forth in the apparatus, he shouted to John to stop. John immediately cut the power and the rod froze into its bent shape (see Fig. 9). John Alexander had previously

---

[14] Pub. Note: US Psychotronics Association (USPA) still holds conferences to this day. Visit www.psychotronics.org for more information.

[15] Pub. Note: Hal Puthoff is a world famous physicist who not only has published seminal papers on zero point energy and other topics in *Physical Review* and other journals, but also worked for the CIA for several years on their Remote Viewing Project which was officially declared a failure in a subsequent CIA report but Hal published a follow-up rebuttal. Hal also independently tested the spoon-bending psychic Uri Geller with Dr. Russell Targ in their lab. Dr. Harold Puthoff is at the Institute for Advanced Studies, 11855 Research Blvd., Austin TX 78759

marked the rod and examined it later to ensure that it could not have been replaced with an identical rod by John. John Alexander did not actually witness the rod being bent.

It was agreed that Pharos should present a proposal for a demonstration of the Hutchison Effect as soon as possible.

Meanwhile, the Murphy's had sold the house and John was told to move by the end of March. John complained of being in a constant state of stress as he had no money to pay for such a large undertaking and, besides, he had nowhere to go. "It would take two months to calibrate the machines! Will Pharos help me out?" At this point Pharos had just about run out of money and the three of us, my father, Alex and myself were providing John with some bare necessities plus some equipment out of our own pockets. First John considered tearing up the Pharos contract and going to the media with his own demonstrations to raise money. The Pharos contract expressly forbade this unless all parties agreed. We were not that desperate yet. A few weeks later John proposed to Pharos to work for free in return for help in moving him to a new location, however, "The royalties and commissions I would like payment [for]."

The whole moving affair was putting a strain on relations between John and Alex.

Nevertheless, John was proceeding with the slow dismantling and packing of the equipment. In describing the phasing and energy reflecting sections of the machine, John stated:

> "The heart of the machine, its Qs, surface[s], all thrown in a box. This is one long set back and yet maybe a blessing. Later on I picture in my mind this unit rebuilt... tuning is important – I would hook it up... so you and I can take notes to get the one in Toronto working,"
>
> "I feel these machines so intensely, I feel almost a component, to see and feel the energy I cannot put into words."

By the end of February, John and Alex had packed up the equipment and were looking for a place to set up the new laboratory. John was feeling increasingly despondent about the future. Even so, he continued to forward diagrams and thoughts about energy devices including a dissimilar metal battery under great spring tension using antimony, bismuth, aluminum and steel. This may have been the precursor of the later "crystal converter". I strongly advised him to sign and date all his drawings, sketches and descriptions for future reference

He was surprised that the INSCOM group had found his technology "...far out..." because he thought that such a group would have had access to much stranger technology than his. This was not so.

I reminded John that we were still trying to raise funds from Canadian sources as well as those in the US even though we had been stung by the failure of the San Diego demonstration. John apologised for the failure "I should have checked the control unit and coil..." and complained about mildew. However, we still paid John his consulting fee for the Galluppi demonstration per the Pharos contract. Feeling contrite about the San Diego non-demo, he demurred: "... indeed I would be happy and honoured to work in your lab [in Toronto]. I don't expect payment at all for ... the San Diego group demo... All future work and consulting time free of charge as long as you want."

I was still attempting to convince John to come to Toronto and either work in my laboratory or we would set him up in his own space. I went on to describe the Toronto laboratory equipment available to him which included:

- 100 kV transformer
- low voltage lab
- 8 foot bed lathe for coil winding etc.

- milling machine to come
- grounded double Faraday cage (steel screen inside Al shell)
- discharge spheres
- 115 kV capacitors
- 100 kV DC supply.

"Like your lab, I have to have [my] setup and have the freedom of an industrial situation not an apartment." [emphasis JHs] This is an interesting statement, for the future was to bring just the opposite. "My décor is a laboratory, an army cot and a hot plate." Later, he reiterated our mutual understanding "I fully understand the importance of Teslian technology and its implications. I hope it does not turn into a military weapon." Pharos had agreed that this was the last thing we wanted as well.

Finally in early April, Alex had found a temporary storage location useful until we could establish the next demonstration location. John found lots of damage to equipment from the move and bemoaned the time it would take to get the system up and running again. He stayed at his friend Brian Borrowdale's home in Vancouver temporarily. Alex was not too happy with the arrangements and problems surfaced about John's rent and who was to pay (Pharos or John). John mentioned having his lawyer, Flynn Marr, set up a trust account for Pharos payments so he could keep his pension. In his depressed state he wrote: "But you see I must do things my way from now on so I won't get into any more messes with false promises, you will find out the truth to all this someday [emphasis JH]... This is my last letter... I always do and still do hold you as my friends." Just what this truth is we are still waiting to find out!

By May, we still hadn't found actual funding but I was continuing to present John's invention in various avenues. In January, Alex and I had formally presented the Hutchison

Effect to Al Holt at NASA; I had presented the concept to Dr. Morgan Raiford in Atlanta, a wealthy ophthalmic surgeon who later assisted funding the Second International Symposium on Non-Conventional Energy Technology; to Dr. Hans Nieper of Germany at a meeting in Madison. WI; at the Portland, OR, meeting of the US Parapsychological Association and at my Second International Symposium on Non-Conventional Energy Technology in Atlanta in September among others.

In early June, I wrote a briefing on the Hutchison Effect for Maj. Gen. Stubblebine and sent it to Washington. This time, with the help of John Alexander, we received a positive response. INSCOM would fund the setting up of John's equipment as long as it was under the guidance of Alex and myself. John reckoned that we could get the system up and running again by August. On June 19th I traveled to Vancouver to assist John and Alex set up the apparatus and perform some preliminary tests.

The building Alex had found was a large concrete warehouse on 141 Riverside Drive which was being used to store some movie props. It had a small concrete room with a mezzanine floor above it which was just the right size for John's equipment (see Fig. 13). Much time was spent trying to convince John to pare down the original equipment to that which was needed for the demonstration. This was quite difficult for John as he was all for continually augmenting the apparatus. Finally, we transported a considerable quantity of his original high-voltage transformers, coils, electrostatic machine, capacitors, etc. to the new location and Alex and I spent several days with John's assistance in assembling the equipment and putting it in the right position and wiring various components together. I say "with John's assistance" because Alex and I wanted to see if we could put the apparatus together according to the circuit diagrams and positions I had drawn for the original apparatus at the Murphy's house. John was interested in this attempt as well. While we wired up the system, John busied himself "rearranging the furniture", i.e. moving some of the major pieces of equipment into positions which, he felt, were better suited to the new room in which we were to do the demonstration. One major difference between the setup at Murphy's and the INSCOM test was the replacement of the 400 kHz CW ("continuous wave") transmitter with a small double-triode (811 tubes) Tesla coil. The other major components were still in operation: large Tesla coil, dual-ended Tesla coil suspended from the ceiling, van de Graaff electrostatic generator, spark gaps across capacitors and high-voltage transformers to power the capacitors, small radioactive source in copper tube, etc.

In order to visualize the extent of the area of "influence", I had constructed a frame of dozens of ping pong balls suspended by threads in a 3-dimensional lattice. Initially this was placed in the active area amidst the equipment, where the balls would bounce and sway violently due to electrostatic forces. This was clearly not going to help, so we placed the frame above the ceiling of the room, on the mezzanine above. Evidently, during some tests at which I was not present, the balls would sway but were not really useful in visualizing the active area.

Alex and I spent considerable time attempting to achieve lift of test objects when John was not present. Although John was fully apprised of our attempts, we did little more than move some light-weight pieces of foam around – nothing that could not be ascribed to electrostatically-induced motion. It was only after John decided to add a few other large metallic masses and construct a few new devices that significant events occurred. These included fixing a large flat spiral coil of copper tubing to one wall and hanging additional coils from the ceiling. Several effects that occurred when I was present were apparently manifest at a considerable distance from the apparatus. At one point a large industrial overhead high-pressure sodium light burst apart. The mirror in the bathroom at least 50 feet away suddenly cracked and a farmer's plough used as a movie prop crashed over onto its side. It was about 75 feet from the active area!

After placing test objects on a plywood platform in the centre of the myriad of pieces of apparatus, the typical warmup schedule involved John turning on the control switches to power the van de Graaff electrostatic machine, the "power supply" for the large Tesla coil, the new small Tesla coil. The phrase "power supply" is in quotations as the Tesla coil was not actually driven in any conventional manner, see Part II. He would always have a long fluorescent light tube in one hand and would probe about in the "hot zone", or the active zone where we expected lift or disruption to occur. Upon dimming the room lights, we would see the tube flicker with light as John probed the zone. He would also generally be wearing earphones connected to a military surplus low frequency receiver nearby to listen for characteristic hisses and crackles of corona discharge. After several minutes to perhaps half an hour of filling the space and covering the equipment with electrostatic charge, he would switch on the power to the high voltage transformers which would charge up several capacitors, some with an air spark gap across them. These would discharge with a very loud BANG and flash of light every 30 – 60 seconds depending on the transformer rating and gap width.

Then he would start the main tuning itself by adjusting the knobs on a high-voltage variable capacitor cabinet (the main "tuning" unit – see Part II) near the entrance to the room. Continually listening on the 'phones, he would make an adjustment and then wait. If he was lucky, or the earth's geomagnetic activity was low, or the humidity was just right or some other unknown factor was within certain limits, something would take off or break apart within 6 to 8 hours. Our goal was to fine-tune the system to whittle that time down to a few hours at most.

John was always very careful to keep himself and others well away from the active area, not only due to the danger of the numerous high voltage devices but also because our presence affected the active area.

In addition to the molybdenum rod sent by John Alexander, many other lifts and fracturing events occurred after the re-construction of the apparatus and before the INSCOM demonstration. I was not present for these events as I had to be attending to matters in Toronto. However, Alex kept me informed about the progress. Both Alex and John were becoming quite excited by the middle of August as the effects were now becoming more frequent. In fact, the system was tuned to a point where after switching on in the morning, effects could be almost guaranteed to occur within a couple of hours. This was the point we were waiting for. We called John Alexander to have the INSCOM team come to Vancouver for a demonstration on August 23 and 24.

I arrived from Toronto late morning and the INSCOM team arrived at the warehouse in the afternoon of the Aug 23. The INSCOM team John Alexander had assembled consisted of himself, John Rink and Bob Freyman, scientists from Los Alamos National Laboratory in New Mexico, Dave Porter from INSCOM itself, Don Stefanik who worked under Porter, and Don Hendrix, an army night vision specialist. Alex and John had been up late the previous evening getting everything in order and hoping the effects could be produced with the required consistency. Due to various competing schedules, the INSCOM team had to fly out later in the afternoon of Aug 24. We had about 24 hours to demonstrate a phenomenon that sometimes took days to appear.

Before the apparatus was turned on, the INSCOM team was invited to inspect all aspects of the equipment as well as areas above the test room and all around it, to ensure no hidden wires, coils magnets, etc. I took them on a small “tour” of the various components of the apparatus and described some of the history of our involvement in the Hutchison Effect. As John started tuning the apparatus, Porter, Stefanik and Hendrix busied themselves getting video camera equipment set up as well as taking notes and drawings of the apparatus.

Rink and Alexander appeared to be the most open-minded of the group. John Rink had brought a newly-acquired Tektronix hand-held portable storage oscilloscope with a small antenna and was sniffing around watching the electric field signals from the Tesla coils on his 'scope, keen to witness and record anything unusual first-hand.

Bob Freyman was clearly the most skeptical of the group. He was apparently the main man that Los Alamos would send to de-bunk claims of "free energy" when Los Alamos was asked to pass judgment. He was continually trying to question me, as the lone engineer/scientist on our team, about the specifics of the operation of the apparatus and in particular how I thought this extremely low-energy apparatus coupled to the earth's gravitational field. To him, the equipment was completely unimpressive and looked as if it "was on loan from a museum." He wanted to know our educational credentials and what theory John or I had come up with to explain the effect. I had not developed any such theory, but suggested that some possibilities existed in the work of Rene-Louis Vallee and others, including even Tom Bearden. We were sinking fast in the estimation of Bob Freyman.

When I was not able to provide a detailed explanation of how the various electric and magnetic fields interacted and why, if they acted individually like normal electric fields, they could collectively create the effects, we hit bottom. Freyman was convinced this experiment was a sham and just another in a series of failed experiments designed to waste "serious scientists' time." He explained with obvious delight how the most famous "free energy" device in recent history was actually a fraud.

This was the famous case of Thomas Henry Moray of Salt Lake City, Utah, (see also Chapter: 1982 above) who had perfected a series of devices in the 1930s – 1950s. These devices evidently extracted considerable energy from a simple single wire antenna and good earth ground. The saga is written up in a book called "The Sea of Energy in Which the Earth Floats".[16] Many demonstrations were given to prominent

[16] Pub. Note: latest edition edited by son John E. Moray, who now also calls himself the author on the cover, is available on Amazon.com. It is worthwhile to search for earlier editions or other books online to learn more original details about the inventor T. Henry Moray and his free energy discovery.

citizens and scientists. One of the most important for validating the operation was carried out in the Utah desert. Evidently, Moray asked a witness to choose a spot at random in the desert for a demonstration and the apparatus was loaded into a car and driven to a spot randomly chosen by the witness. According to the normal operation of the device, a short wire antenna was put up and connected to the antenna terminal of the device. A good earth ground was made by hammering at least one rod into the earth and connecting it to the ground terminal of the device. Lo and behold! After a short time spent tuning, enough electricity was produced to power several light bulbs and other electrical loads the witness brought along. All as Moray had claimed.

Freyman, however, related that, unbeknownst to the witness, Moray had earlier secretly outfitted a welding truck with a gas or diesel-powered generator for producing large electric currents through the ground. There must also have been a silencing device on the engine. On the day of the demonstration, Moray had instructed his confederate to drive the welding truck a safe distance behind Moray's car and stay out of sight. When Moray's car stopped, the truck also stopped and large grounding stakes were driven into the earth from which large cables were connected to the generator. The large ground currents produced by the generator were picked up by Moray's device and converted into apparent "free energy".

I personally doubt the accuracy of this story and as an electrical engineer find it hard to fathom some technical aspects of the explanation, including the demonstration aboard an aircraft.

Back in Vancouver, the cameras were rolling and the oscilloscopes were glowing and the capacitors were discharging and the van de Graaff machine was hissing and John was fussing. Time went on. Nothing was happening. Sandwiches were consumed and Bob Freyman's grin was getting bigger. Alex and I were growing more and more concerned. Around dinner time, something did happen – a high-voltage transformer suddenly quit. John shut everything off. We realized that there was no spare transformer and that no junk yards were still open. I set to work opening the transformer to see if it was salvageable. Several hours later, I had repaired it and we started again. However, it was growing late and the rest of the INSCOM team was becoming agitated. Freyman was letting everyone know his opinion and at his urging, we all packed up late that night, having witnessed nothing out of the ordinary except a camera cable overheating and a frustrated engineer trying to fix a high-voltage transformer.

Although we attempted another demonstration the next morning, most of the party had to leave early in the afternoon. I was extremely disappointed. Alex and John were completely dejected after all their work, and we begged at least some of the INSCOM folk to stay one more day. This was not to be. They left empty-handed with nothing to show for their time and effort, and all but Rink and Alexander thinking the demonstration was mostly a waste of time, just as Bob Freyman had predicted.

A few weeks later, John Alexander expressed his conviction that something unusual must have been going on based on the molybdenum rod and maintained his faith that we were not trying to perpetrate a scientific fraud. He still keeps that faith to this day. Recently he confided that he had asked each of the five scientists what they personally thought after the failed demonstration. All but Freyman stated that they believed something unique had happened – only it did not happen during the demonstration. "Only Freyman was highly negative, and unexplainably, irrationally so." He went on to remind me that there was a room beside the demonstration room which was locked. Freyman was convinced that we had hidden a high-energy device there which was used somehow to cause the effects. He was proven wrong when someone showed up with the key and the room proved nearly empty.

The official report of the demonstration originated with Los Alamos National Laboratory and was sent to the Army. The implication is that Freyman wrote the report as he was the senior scientist at the demonstration. Apparently Rink had little to say in the matter. The report was derogatory and highly critical of the experimental setup and especially our (my) inability to propose any coherent theory as to why the device did as it was purported to have done. A month after the demonstration, John Hutchison asked Pharos for a copy of the videos taken by the INSCOM team. John Alexander told us that nothing was seen on the films and that he was quite disappointed by the whole episode. Evidently the report was later destroyed according to standard policy, and the video tapes either reused or destroyed. I believe John Alexander when he says that no copies of any report or videotapes are still available.

In a letter of October 10 from John Hutchison to Norm Hathaway, John recalled that prior to the INSCOM demonstration, he and Alex were witnessing good lift and disruption effects within 35 feet of the active area several times a day: "good effect on ring … row of light bulbs blew out … ping pong balls sway … old plow thrown over … cup overturned as George saw [during initial setup]." However, he bemoaned the transformer failure and especially Bob Freyman's disparaging comments. Perhaps significantly, he mentioned that two close friends who were in the surplus electronics business and major suppliers to John had unexpectedly died shortly before the demonstration. To top it off, his mother had also just passed away! He went on "Also I am, I believe, having unconscious "bouts" of telekinetic problems as electrical machines are affected [this effect started in about May, 1983]. If they persist, I would seek help." It may be inferred from these passages that part of the reason for the failed demonstration was the subconscious mental state that John found himself in prior to and during the demonstration.

After the INSCOM non-demonstration, when not depressed, John seemed keen to set up the next laboratory (number 3) "to clear my name." This was to be primarily a public relations vehicle for John to show the world, via television, that these effects were real. He suggested that Pharos back out of our contract as

> "...it costs money and headaches – too high risk... it is only a money-waster since Pharos cannot afford to waste money on a venture that twice [emphasis John's] disappointed all concerned. I wish to make a living and rid myself of this pension. Inventions are a dead end street; even this phenomenon "LID" would not even make a good side show as it stands now."

An additional reason for John wanting to extract himself from the Pharos contract was that the BC government was threatening to cut off his pension due to his consulting work for Pharos. My father wrote back that we were still committed to continuing to try to raise funds for "the most important technical endeavour that we should support." He went on to remind John of contract commitments and against arbitrary public demonstrations "until we think there is adequate security for you and the technology". Pharos was worried that others might try to steal the technology for nefarious purposes.

As our short-term lease had expired after the INSCOM fiasco, Alex helped John set up shop in the basement of a store on 3744 E. Hastings in Burnaby, BC. It was here that John started to seriously add components to the apparatus in an attempt to improve the intensity and frequency of the events. This was the place where John set a nearby telephone pole behind the basement swaying so much that it attracted a crowd of onlookers. Apparently the sway was close to 3 feet at the top. It was feared that the wires would snap.

John was now wanting to perform public demonstrations to vindicate himself and attract funding since Pharos was having trouble arranging same after two failed demonstrations. In particular, he had made contact with BCTV's Alyn Edwards for whom he did eventually make a demonstration of a heavy piece of foam rubber levitating. He wanted Pharos to relax the restriction set out in the contract for no outside demonstrations unless we all agreed. This we were not prepared to do just yet as Alex had contacted the Canadian military through the Defence Research Board in Ottawa.

Throughout all this John was still fascinated with the Moray, Hendershot and other free energy devices. He was continually forwarding to me sketches of various forms of "Moray Engines". I had invited the French physicist Rene-Louis Vallee to speak at the First International Symposium in Toronto. He explained his theories about how electron-positron pair creation from the "diffuse energy of space" (which we might now term the Zero Point Energy[17]) could lead to gravitational effects. These concepts I had introduced to John early in our relationship and they held a great fascination for him. He was also continuing to study the theories of Tom Bearden. Sometime in 1983, Tom had written a monograph entitled "Creation of Magnetic Monopoles" after I had told Tom about John's anomalous magnetization experiment. This occurred in 1981 during one of his attempts at levitating several objects including a flat machinist's file. The 10 inch long file did not levitate but broke into 4 roughly equally-sized pieces. This was caught on one of our early 8 mm movie films. While trying to put the file pieces back together, Alex and John discovered that the pieces would repel each other at their mutual break. This is anomalous behavior as normally, breaking a bar magnet into pieces results in the pieces attracting each other. To Tom, this was clear evidence of John having produced three such strong magnetic monopolar regions that the file just split apart. Tom hypothesized that pure magnetic force was generated at a distance using coherent interference of two or more beams of scalar waves which John apparently produced with his apparatus.

---

[17] Pub. Note: See *Zero Point Energy: the Fuel of the Future* by Thomas Valone, Integrity Research Institute Publishers, 2007, available on Amazon.com

I still have that file in my possession although it has been handled enough that this strange magnetic effect is now only very weak.

Tom had been working closely with Joe Jahoda, founder of the Astron Corporation, a US company specializing in radio antenna design and testing. Alex and I had hoped for some funding from Astron via Tom, but none was forthcoming.

Here John Hutchison is holding one of the more perplexing pieces of merged metal possibly called "disruption." A butter knife had lodged itself inside a block of aluminum during a high voltage session and it was not clear what happened to the knife until the aluminum block was sawed in half to reveal the knife intact and tightly embedded in the metal block, as if the aluminum had become soft for a time allowing the knife to slip inside. – Pub. Note

An even better photo, from an online Hutchison video, of the one of a kind butter knife in aluminum merging seen on the previous page, after shaving the top layer of aluminum away to reveal the presence of the knife intact on the inside. Unfortunately, some of the knife has also been cut away which now appears flush with the aluminum surface. This is only due to the careless machining of the aluminum in overzealous eagerness to find out what was inside. – Pub. Note

1984: John and the Media

The New Year started off with John somewhat depressed about the way things had been going. In a March letter to Pharos, he mentioned that he had done a TV interview but did not reveal any of the actual workings of the apparatus. He wanted to do more high-voltage "Tesla Lab" demonstrations: "...looks like there is a future in this... I never was an inventor, I only liked to play with nature's energies. [Things] have not progressed anywhere and... the novelty of the [LID] device has worn off... I never again want to see repeats of San Diego or August 1983 Riverside Drive [demonstrations] where a group of people came [to] see something and NOTHING HAPPENS [emphasis JH]."

In an uncanny fulfillment of the "prophesy" of Bob Freyman, John stated that he wanted to set up a turn of the century (ca. 1900) electrical museum for Vancouver's Expo '86 and asked Pharos for paid work to manufacture any parts that we might be needing for other projects. The only projects underway at the time for Pharos were the Hutchison Effect and Alex's Hydrocarbon Detector, which I was working on and which did not require machining.

Meanwhile, John was also courting other possible investors including one Daniel C. LaFlamme who was involved in "megaprojects for inventors and has a huge lab." Nothing came of this as LaFlamme bad-mouthed Alex behind his back. John told him to "shove off with his 25 million."

By December, John had made various changes and additions to the apparatus after obtaining much more surplus high-voltage equipment, including:

- 1 m diameter double loop coils at low DC voltage
- different static generator
- 150 kV DC unit
- new deep ground.

With this he was able to get more control and some slow lifting events as in the earlier experiments in the Murphy's basement. Now he was going to put on a demonstration for CTV of "...only Tesla's high voltage research and not the lift...this way I cannot jeopardize Pharos position. No lift demonstration." According to John, it was necessary to get the Hutchison Effects more consistent rather than to make a duplicate device in Toronto. He wanted to get a new lab space as he was finding problems with people walking around upstairs in the store and upsetting the apparatus.

During this time, the existing Pharos contract lapsed. John was now excited about more TV demonstrations. In a telephone conversation with Alex in early December, I learned that CTV, a Canada-wide television corporation, did send a crew to videotape John's apparatus as he had previously arranged. John initially was not going to show a lift event, however, after spending two days filming, they finally captured some effects on tape. A long 15 x 10 inch piece of heavy foam rubber (approx 5 pounds in weight) achieved a slow lift, aluminum foil was bent up, wires of the apparatus were bouncing around and a file broke. No major disruptions took place but evidently, the film crew was astounded

As was usually the case, John did not witness these events personally as he was busy adjusting various knobs and dials, eyes fixed on indicators, all the while concentrating on the sounds of the apparatus via headphones. His new setup, crowded as ever, prevented his direct viewing of the active area. This was not such a drawback as it might first appear, as effects could occur almost anywhere in the immediate vicinity of the basement.

Alex further related that John was using his old van de Graaff electrostatic machine, improved to provide 250,000 volts potential, a "dual-tuned" circuit and large magnetic loops all in a triangular configuration, with the active area in the centre). On the second day of taping, a high-voltage power supply powering a simple air spark gap failed, halting the demonstration.

The CTV show's producer, a friend of John's, asked Alex to help edit the footage for broadcast. It was shown on the local CTV network station in British Columbia, BCTV's "Newshour" on December 12, 1984. During conversations with Alex, John admitted that he "...wants only to work with Pharos." With that in mind, we quickly drafted another agreement for John's perusal and left it with him to think about. Meanwhile, Alex had been in touch with John Alexander about the possibility of another demonstration to John Alexander. John Alexander stated that the BCTV show might just help the Pharos project as it was the first time that completely neutral parties had witnessed and filmed significant events. Alex and I were not so sure, as we figured that the public exposure could bring a rash of interest both from those interested in stealing the technology as well as those possibly bent on shutting us down, perhaps for national security reasons.

1985: Jack Houck and Psychokinesis

In a January telephone conversation with John, he told me that many people had been contacting him and BCTV about the demonstration aired a few weeks prior. People had found John's location and were dropping in hoping to see a demonstration. The network was receiving several calls a week and its parent network, CBC (Canadian Broadcasting Corporation) was interested in "doing a show". This was the kind of thing we were trying to prevent. It would detract from the scientific study of the effect and turn it into a public show. Ever-increasing interest worldwide would snowball into a requirement for John to satisfy the public's thirst for spectacle, rather than trying to develop it into something useful. On the other hand, we saw John's frustration at having two failed private demonstrations but a successful public demonstration. Naturally, he had wanted to vindicate himself in front of Pharos and the world. To the extent that the BCTV broadcast attracted so many interested parties, he succeeded.

He further related a story about his creation of ball lightning a few days before. The day was typically British Columbia January, cold, foggy, with drizzle and high humidity. John had just completed his new van de Graaff machine which featured a 24 inch dome, 9 – 10 feet high, with a 6 inch wide belt. In ideal (dry) conditions, it could produce 500 – 600 thousand volts. According to John, a 5 inch diameter "fireball" originated near a 200 kilovolt transformer. He heard a slight crackling sound and described the ball as silver-white with a slight bluish tint. It also appeared opaque and cast a shadow. It flew slowly around in an arc amongst the apparatus until it hit a grounded wire about 8 feet above the floor. The wire wiggled a bit as the ball disappeared. The whole event lasted 8 – 10 seconds.

John said he had met a Professor Sterling of Simon Fraser University who evidently knew just what John was doing with respect to ball lightning.

Later in the month, in another telephone conversation, John was bemoaning his lab space – the rent had been increased, electricity was too expensive and he was having problems with insurance. The building of which he occupied the basement had new owners who now wanted the basement as well. He was concerned that he would have to sell some equipment to pay for the increases, as no new deal had been struck with Pharos at that time. I sent him some money to cover a few month's rent and operating costs in the meantime. It was at this time that the term "Hutchison Effect" was coined by Alex Pezarro.

He described how a week before, he had placed a circular conical hard steel bushing in the active area. It was about 3 inches tall and 3 inches at the base, tapering to about 1 ½ inches at the top with a hole drilled through the length. I still have it in my possession. According to John, during lift experiments, he detected a "field" about 2 ½ feet above the table on which the various samples, including the bushing, were placed. It "wavered" above the samples and then "hit" the bushing which fell apart with a metallic "crinkling" sound. This was similar to the sound that the Galluppis, Alex and I heard when we witnessed a bushing cracking in November 1982.

An April letter to Pharos from John noted that he was getting more serious about continuing with Pharos as he was:

"...tired of all the street people who do not have a clue...As Alex has pointed out: 'What do I want?' Basically a proper building... plus a contract to protect yourselves and myself... plus I really want [to interact] with the scientific community. My dream [is] to see this technology for the space program and an alternate source of power."

And mentioned wanting a new contract with Pharos.

Later that month, John telephoned me worried again about paying the rent in a few months and maybe having to move. He had received a letter of support from Elizabeth Rauscher[18] and William Tiller[19] and mentioned a group in the US, possibly associated with them, coming for a visit shortly. They claimed to have $2 million available contingent on a demonstration but wanted to deal with John directly, not going through Pharos. Evidently, they were concerned about John "rotting away" without a proper laboratory and facilities. So were we! Nothing came of that overture, and later both Rauscher and Tiller would find themselves in dire financial straits.

By mid-year, we still had no prospects for solid funding and had been supporting John to the best of our personal abilities. John wrote to my father saying he had considered scrapping all the electrical equipment and keeping just the lathes and machine tools "...so I can make a clean break psychologically." It turned out that John could never make a

---

[18] Pub. Note: Dr. Rauscher was the first female to receive a Ph.D. in physics from UC Berkley and became famous for her physics papers, ELF earthquake prediction patented instrument, as well as her research into remote viewing. Dr. Rauscher also contributed a wireless power transmission chapter to *Harnessing the Wheelwork of Nature: Tesla's Science of Energy*, ed. by Thomas Valone, Adv. Unlim. Pub., 2003

[19] Pub. Note: Dr. Tiller, Engineering Professor Emeritus from Stanford University, is famous for his scientifically-proven, repeatable, psychokinesis experiments under controlled conditions, see *Conscious Acts of Creation*, Pavior Pub., 2001; *Psychoenergetic Science*, Pavior, 2007; *Science and Human Transformation*, Pavior, 1997; and *Some Science Adventures with Real Magic*, Pavior, 2005

clean break as the apparatus and the Hutchison Effect were to become his personal albatross.

Meanwhile, he had improved the stability of the apparatus enough to demonstrate an effect every night. This was the most consistent long-term operation that he had been able to obtain. We were still pressing him to assist us in Toronto to replicate the effect in my laboratory so we could prove that he didn't have to be physically present for the Effect to be seen. In response to this, John wrote on June 10:

> "I do understand your great interest in reproduction of this effect. By the sounds of things [you hope] this effect can somehow be done without my help. Best of luck. Frankly I doubt it. Also if a scientific team was ever formed, I will not guarantee a duplicate model could work."

John went on to relate that he had received some money from Tom Bearden and that Tom wanted John to come to Huntsville but did not have the money to pay for the trip. In the meantime, we had been paying many of John's living expenses, for which he thanked us in a letter in September. He also planned to perform a metal disintegration and lift effects on another TV demonstration for Alyn Edwards who, he said, would have to learn how to operate the device to get maximum effect. It was not clear whether John implied that Alyn could do the entire demonstration by himself. From John's other writings, this was highly unlikely.

In August, another important figure in John's life was introduced to us by John Alexander. This was the scientist Jack Houck[20] who worked for but did not represent McDonnell

---

[20] Pub. Note: The US Psychotronics Association (USPA) is one of the best sources of information on Jack Houck from their conferences when they sponsored Jack Houck's spoon bending classes also called "PK Parties" several times from the late

Douglas aircraft company. Jack had been following closely recent developments in parapsychology, especially those areas involved with the ability of the human consciousness to affect physical objects. He was one of the first to have "spoon-bending parties" at which various pieces of metal kitchenware were deformed apparently by mind power alone.

Alex told John about Jack's work and interest and arranged for Jack to visit John early in the summer. John was delighted to show Jack the setup and a few small effects were demonstrated. Jack's visit inspired John to renew his desire to explore the science of his invention. John stated "All that is needed is the proper set of frequencies to produce the effect." John and Jack discussed the possible psychokinetic aspects of the effect and Jack wrote a short report about his visit (available in footnote 5). It stressed the need to keep an open mind about the possibility that the apparatus was acting as a psychokinetic amplifier in some way, allowing John's innate psychokinetic abilities to be manifest on a large scale.

According to Alex, many effects were occurring outside the active area which Jack and Alex could hear but not see immediately. After Jack's visit, we gave John a video camera with the intention of setting it up to catch a wide view while John concentrated on the tuning. Unfortunately, John seemed more interested in focusing in on the details of the object or objects to be lifted or disrupted. While this was useful in showing the metal deformation, it was problematic when the objects suddenly shot out of camera range. It also fuelled speculation that John faked the films and videos.

In letters from the latter part of the year he stated that he thought that the effect might never have been discovered in other circumstances: "Thank goodness I was not contaminated with orthodox physics." In an apparent confirmation of this observation, he went on to describe improvements to the old lift system of the Murphy's basement and the INSCOM demonstration:

1980s through 2004 (DVDs are available). Visit www.psychotronics.org and www.jackhouck.com for more information and online PK Party videos.

- "Control factor on H. Effect mass problem solved. Consistency solved on light objects and heavy objects focus system... better, control on metal breakup 50 percent more accurate."
- "Low voltage x strong magnetic field – high voltage x 5 cps low magnetic [field?] – ground plane – fixed permanent magnetic fields strong variable [?] – variable cps dual magnetic fields..."
- "static control focus unit DC – HF AC mixer field shaper, electrostatic wave projector stationary pointed to target area..."
- "Nuclear source now with proper field shaping units"
- "400 Kc now eliminated replaced by S band 2500 – 3500 Mc variable field projector and 2500 Kc wideband generator – Tesla Coil."
- "DC supply replaced – 0 to 150 kV DC "
- "cascade discharge [in capacitors] from no. 1 cap to no. 4 in DC storage steps until breakdown."
- "Most transformers replaced with 200kV using interferometer effect [?] introduction to ring system."
- "will replace old neon sign transformers with 6 – 150,000 V as neon sign transformers are a hindrance."
- "[Improve] front end of system iron core [choke] coil with power factor capacitor [for] proper voltage stabilization to all components with override switch." (Note in Jun 10 '85 letter "Even the faintest adjustment makes it more active or not work at all.")

- "Ballast system – now all replaced with variable ballast, multiple ballast, through tuning unit and now fixed tuned units."
- "All equipment ruggedized for all-day operation. Fine tuned some of the old components."
- "Will incorporate large static machine with various multiple taps [i.e. corona rings] with direct connections to proper electrostatic pulsed balls…"
- "More tank circuits."
- "Low voltage DC supply now applied to magnetron and nuclear source."
- "Will replace one spark gap system with tube system and incorporate X-band RADAR generator as field is still weak and is too random."
- monitoring equipment includes spectrum analysis, field strength meters, Q meters, low-frequency dual trace tracking system [?].

John's confidence in the apparatus was growing. He stated: "The field matrix is many times improved as all I have to do is turn the device on and she starts up with frequencies that produce a slight lift effect and with a burst of heavy lifts…The device as it stands now will function every time I turn it on - guaranteed. [emphasis JH] The metal breakup is just a low band system I have only partial control over…The target area is U – shaped, ends at the walls, expands and contracts with long distance projections up to 200 feet away."

In October, John gave a small demonstration to Bill Ross and Brian Borrowdale. By this time, Bill was becoming fearful of the device, not only for its potentially destructive nature, but also probably for what he saw it doing to John, turning him into a more publicity-seeking individual from the reclusive tinkerer he had known. Bill even wrote a report of his observations dated October 14 (available in footnote 5).

On October 21, Norm Hathaway had an opportunity to visit John for a few hours during a business trip to see the apparatus and, it was hoped, see a demonstration of the effects. Unfortunately, he only was able to stay long enough to see some small electrostatic effects, notwithstanding John's considerable confidence in the device repeatability on demand. Norm complained about feeling slightly ill at ease during the demonstration as if the field was affecting him somehow. John also mentioned that during my father's visit, he (John) also felt dizzy for a time. Perhaps this is what Bill Ross was concerned about as well.

Throughout the year, John had been plagued by nosy neighbours interested in either seeing demonstrations or trying to have John evicted. Alyn Edwards had to write to the Tenant Action Centre on behalf of John, vouching for John's character. Pharos had not been asleep either, continually trying to raise funds for John even though there had been no formal agreement between it and John for some time. Alex had found an interested ear in Maj. Tim Dear of the Canadian Armed Forces in Ottawa. He had suggested that we contact the Canadian Directorate for Science, Technology and Industry (DSTI) in particular, Dr. Lorne Kuehn. This Alex did and after sending an information package we had a meeting with Dr. Kuehn and Tim Dear. They agreed to come out to Vancouver in early 1986 to see a demonstration of the Hutchison Effect. Alex was hoping that they might assist in a program for the development of the Hutchison Effect for defensive purposes while allowing us to develop commercial civilian applications. After the INSCOM fiasco, I wasn't sure that this would obtain, even if we had made a successful demonstration. However, it was the only solid lead we had come across in many months.

1986: The DSTI/Canadian Military Demonstration

In mid-1985, I had started to consult with a Toronto group called Mega Research, headed by Mr. Laszlo ('Leslie') I. Szabo. The stated aim of this research was to verify by experiment Szabo's electrical engineering calculations concerning the possibility of extracting energy from permanent magnets. This involved designing, building and testing many electrical generators, both direct current (DC) and alternating current (AC), in a very short time. This was because Szabo had raised considerable funds from a Canadian Government program designed to promote energy innovation via tax credits that could be bought and sold in order to fund the research. Although this was the stated aim of the program, it was often abused by those wishing to make a fast dollar without doing credible work.

Szabo had convinced Professor Martin Muldoon of York University in Toronto that a small portion of his equations relating to magnetic fields interacting with passive circuit elements (capacitors, inductors and resistors) was correct. With this assurance, he claimed, contrary to thermodynamic law, that the entire set of equations validated his view that certain electrical and magnetic circuits could be used to extract energy from steady magnetic fields. With this in hand, he amassed considerable funds and hired my services to assist in putting his ideas into practice. In addition, he purchased some of my older test equipment and set up a laboratory first in downtown Toronto, then in Mississauga, a city outside of Toronto. Eventually, Alex came to assist for several months. Naturally, we tried to interest Szabo in funding the further development of the Hutchison Effect. He showed considerable interest and made a verbal commitment to put up some money if we could hammer out a joint agreement between Pharos, Mega and John.

Meanwhile, DSTI was planning to arrive at the end of March and Alex was busy helping John get ready for the demonstration. Apparently, John was "up" for this one. The demonstration started in the afternoon of March 23 and ended in the late afternoon of March 24. In attendance were Dr. Kuehn, together with Dr. Lokken, Harold Wilson, Lt. Col. Larsen, Alex Pezarro and myself. This team was less interested in the electromagnetic aspects than the INSCOM team as they were not as well equipped with analytical equipment. They were, however, well equipped with photographic and video equipment, as well as open minds. Unlike Bob Freyman, they were approaching this phenomenon with positive expectations. Unfortunately, this positive mindset was not enough to guarantee a successful demonstration. It was a failure. Only a couple of very minor movements were witnessed, easily ascribable to electrostatic events.

Again, Alex and I were very disappointed to the point of "throwing in the towel". Surprisingly, John did not seem very upset. He was confident that there would be some levitation showing up on the DSTI videotapes. The DSTI team was also disappointed but did not cast aspersions on the whole affair. Dr. Kuehn in effect said to call him when we get the phenomenon more repeatable. This after Alex and John had been getting good effects several times per hour in the days preceding the demonstration!

Two days after this latest "non-event", John wrote to Pharos in Toronto thanking Dr. Kuehn and his team for their interest and noting their concern for better reproducibility. John needed input on this problem and suggested perhaps Dr. Rauscher or Prof. Sterling might be able to help. With regard to his state of mind during the demonstration: "...I felt good with you guys..." indicating perhaps that his conscious state had little to do with the failure of the demonstration this time. He went on to state: "I do hope the videos turn up some levitation..." This statement confirmed what all had agreed, namely that no Hutchison Effect levitation has been eye-witnessed.

During the Spring, at his request, I was supplying Dr. Kuehn with material relevant to the Hutchison Effect, including additional photographs of early levitations, background science and samples of metal. He was in the process of writing up his report and these materials were of use to him in drawing conclusions in the absence of photographic evidence. Also at this time, Alex and I were trying to solidify funding from Mega Research but becoming increasingly uneasy about dealing with Szabo.

Sometime earlier, John had received several telephone calls and inquiries from 'foreigners' as he described them. One was traced to the Yugoslav Trade Mission. He alerted his Member of Parliament, Chuck Cook, who wrote back that that "Because this is a matter involving national security..." the foreign telephone calls issue should be handled by the Canadian Security and Intelligence Service (CSIS). There was no national security issue concerning John's experiments, only the possible foreign inquiries.

On June 9, I received a letter from Dr. Kuehn plus his "Trip Report". In a sentence, Dr. Kuehn summed up the report's findings: "We do not see any further consideration of support to your endeavour until such time as you can assure a reproducible effect..." He mentioned a metallurgical report sent to me based on the sample I had previously supplied. This metallurgical report I sent along to Alex for discussion with John. John responded in a handwritten note: "JH. I fully agree to this [Kuehn's] letter."

A month later John wrote from 675 E. 5th St. where he and Bill Ross were living together of his concern that Alex was not pushing hard enough to obtain the film and video footage taken during the DSTI visit. During this time, he had no doubt been admonished by his friends that there was actually something demonstrated but was being suppressed by "the Government". Certainly Alex and I were disappointed and Alex was likely complaining vociferously to John about yet another failed demonstration. However, both Alex and I concurred with the DSTI conclusions. In a response prompted primarily out of maintenance of self-esteem, John stated "I realized this [problem] and never allowed full information [about the Hutchison Effect] to be released." The "problem" referred to here is the assumption that there would be activity actually caught on videos etc. but never confirmed by the requisite authorities after the fact. This would therefore allow these authorities to proceed with their own development of the Hutchison Effect without the need to further involve John (or ourselves). Armed with video documentation, John would have the ammunition he needed to argue for continued funding. This concern festered in John and provided added impetus to his desire to get out of Canada and pursue his experimentation in Europe. John was not entirely bitter about the experience, as he wrote "I would like to thank you for your support in the past." In fact, Alex and John were interviewed on CBC TV in February of the next year.

In August Alex and I resigned from Mega Research. Not only had Szabo been pursuing increasingly questionable research projects but we found out that the firm was under investigation by the Canadian tax authorities for alleged tax fraud. This effectively killed the contract we had been negotiating with Mega Research to support John. It was the last formal agreement between John and Pharos. John was on his own. This did not prevent him from seeking advice from Alex and myself on many topics for many years thereafter.

Szabo moved his operation from Canada to Hungary and set up GammaManager Kft in Budaors (see www.gammamanager.com) where he claims to be producing free energy generators.

Evidently, the letter John sent to Chuck Cook prompted Cook to enquire about our demonstration to DSTI. The result was an "Aide Memoire" written by Lt. Col. Larsen dated Nov 12 which concluded "The post-demonstration analysis concluded that the Hutchison apparatus and phenomena were of little scientific or practical value." A letter to Cook from the Minister of National Defence, Perrin Beatty, stated that "A copy of the visit report and some still photography [note: NO videos or films] were provided to Mr. George Hathaway... The video-tape and film were of extremely poor quality and were of no value." According to the DSTI the poor quality of the video was due to interference from the apparatus. I had already given the report to Alex which he later forwarded to John.

Towards the end of the year, John was in touch with Roland Bredow in Germany about making arrangements to get John over to Europe. In Hannover, Dr. Nieper was still promoting novel and exotic energy and propulsion techniques. Evidently, Mel Winfield had contacted Dr. Nieper and was feeding him disinformation according to John which John was at pains to rectify. Getting to Europe would have the additional benefit to John of correcting misapprehensions on the part of European scientists as to the "true" nature of the experiments.

1987: John in Europe I

On Jan 27, Lorne Kuehn sent John a letter thanking him for his letter(s) received via Chuck Cook which were looking for copies of the videos, etc. Kuehn included a few photos from his visit, mostly group shots of the Canadian team outside the building where the demonstration was done but nothing about the tests themselves. He ended the letter "...I hope that you can reproduce your findings..." Another letter to John from Dr. Kuehn later in the Fall thanked John once again for his letters and mentioned that he was impressed with how much John was able to do with military surplus, although he personally had not witnessed the claimed effects.

The following month, in order to try once again to drum up support for John, Alex and John were interviewed by a local TV station. However, nothing of consequence resulted and after cutting formal ties with Pharos, John teamed up with George Liszicasz and Alexander Shereshevsky whom he had met through a surplus electronics dealer. These men established a small company, Axon General Systems and apparently gave John the title of President. John was told that they were partially funded by Boeing Aircraft through someone named Kovaks although this was highly unlikely. Their main goal was not scientific research but making lots of money fast on the Hutchison Effect. They set John up in a small laboratory and started pressing John to produce the effect on demand.

Soon John started to feel trapped. However, during this period (late 1987 – 1989), he filmed some of the most impressive videos of lifting, metal deformation, and other unusual phenomena. Evidently, George and Alexander tried to operate the apparatus themselves with little success (see late 1988 letters). However, they did succeed in blowing up a transformer containing PCBs. This was to be a major blow to John.

Much of 1987 was spent by John trying to arrange tests of his metal samples in Germany through Roland Bredow and another contact, Bruno Bachmann. These people arranged to get some of the samples analysed at the Max Planck Institute in Germany. According to our early XRF (X-Ray Fluorescence) and Electron Micro Probe analyses, there seemed to be an unusual agglomerating effect of the Hutchison Effect on alloying elements in metals, especially aluminum. These elements seemed to come out of solid solution in the metal at the grain boundaries and form globules containing the alloying elements at the fracture points. This was of interest to the German researchers as was the precise nature of the fracturing.

In addition, John was trying to negotiate a contract with Bredow. One such model contract had a 3 year renewable lifetime with the option for John to quit after 1 year. The cost of setting up the laboratory was estimated at close to $CAN 500,000. The letters indicate a young Bredow having recently moved away from his parents' house, working computer sales temporarily while he waited to get his main job with which he hoped to partially finance John's European adventure. Alex tried to warn John that if he was to make a major move, to Europe for example, he would need to have a firmer financial situation when he got there. At that point, however, John's mind was made up and he went.

In a letter from Bredow to John from Nov 22, the results of initial tests at the Max Planck Institute were relayed to John. These results were presented simply in a letter including statements such as "...your samples were destroyed by a very high energy of an implosion...The metal (aluminum samples) is very unusual, not able to be reproduced exactly in Germany but appears close to an aircraft alloy of aluminum." It was not stated exactly who in the Institute did the actual analysis. Bredow went on to mention a conference in Mainz at which John's work was to be discussed. Apparently, two facilities had been contracted to examine the samples: Max Planck and the Bundesanstalt fur Materialforschung und Prufung (Materials Testing Institute – BAM). He also stated that he wanted control over the progress of the project, a reasonable request if he was arranging financing, but needed assurance that no other place on the planet could have produced these effects before expending the energy getting the project off the ground. Hence his concerns about materials testing. He must have been satisfied with the test results for he went on to assist John in getting to Germany shortly thereafter.

Bredow also mentioned that Jeane Manning of Vancouver was assisting John in arranging his voluminous documents. John had met Jeane in 1986. A short time before this, John had also met Elektra Briggs who lived in Philadelphia at the time and was writing about and preparing documentaries on various New Age activities and unusual energy devices such as that of Joseph Newman. Upon seeing the videos of the Hutchison Effect she offered to be John's publicity agent.

1988: "Levitating Cannonball" Video

In January, John sent a letter to me requesting a copy of an 8 mm film we had made during the demonstration to Filippo Galluppi. This I sent to him. In addition, John mentioned that he had sent Bredow the actual sample I had filmed fracturing during Galluppi's visit (see Fig. 8). I have never seen that piece of metal again. John noted how impressed he was with the German analysis and appreciation of the effect and that they seemed to understand more than their North American counterparts: a prophet not appreciated in his own land. I had asked John whether I could give a presentation on the effect at a conference sponsored by the Planetary Association for Clean Energy (PACE) in June 1988 and John was delighted to give his assent. He went on to describe making a 5 lb device (perhaps "Crystal Converter") producing "100 microamps ...with no coils or antennae" and being the result of his investigations into the Moray device.

The following month, John received a letter from Lorne Kuehn, enclosing a metallurgical analysis on samples provided by John and myself to the Department of National Defense. This was in part due to Alex not immediately giving John a copy of the report and some general photographs that Dr. Kuehn had sent to me previously which I forwarded to Alex to give to John. Apparently John had become impatient and asked for a copy for himself. I do not know if Alex had made a copy for John before he got his own. John asked me to send Roland Bredow some metal samples in my possession which I did on February 15.

An April letter to John from Maj. Tim Dear thanked John for his numerous letters and described how he was leaving the Canadian Forces to pursue private interests in technology. He stated that these might even involve the Hutchison Effect in the future. I contacted Maj. Dear in August, 2003 and he still was fascinated with the entire Hutchison affair.

Back in Germany at a conference in Berlin on exotic energy technology, Bredow and a Mr. Amon from BAM were giving a lecture including highlights from the analyses of John's metal samples. At that meeting was Dr. Peter Kokoshinegg from Salzburg, Austria, lecturing on Kirlian photography and the structure of water. John and Dr. Kokoshinegg would have many future dealings. Also in attendance were Stefan Marinov, Gottfried Hilscher, Stefan Hartmann, Herrn Haberle and Volkrodt and representatives from the Methernitha religious commune. All of these people were involved in the search for free energy in Europe in one way or another. John was greatly influenced by the rather freer European spirit of inquiry into exotic ideas than he had found in North America.

Sometime in mid-1988 John met Yin Gazda, a filmmaker who would be his girlfriend for several years.

John was back in Vancouver (at 675 East 5th) in the autumn. He had been in touch with Jack Houck. Even though he generally downplayed the idea of a psychokinetic explanation for the Hutchison Effect, he stated in a letter to me "As you know, the effect was explained by Jack Houck."

In a letter to me from October, he stated that "The system is running again OK" and further that he could not give the precise location of the lab "…as it's very serious now and there have been agents trying to get a view." Also that "The equipment has gone through many stages of development… better approach [now] to equipment layout and proper mass and…nuclear section...The nuclear part plays more of a role than realized." John thanked me for the presentation I gave on his work and the support I encouraged at the PACE conference in June as well as for forwarding copies of some general photos taken by Kuehn et al during the last demonstration. He mentioned that he had not heard from Alex in over a year and a half. He was still very much in contact with his new European friends who were keen to give their verbal support and explanations.

In September, John purchased a used Sony black and white video recorder. This was a large, heavy and unwieldy camera with which John was to take some of his most impressive videos. Unfortunately, he usually operated it without a tripod and in closeup mode which made later analysis very difficult.

Although he had been seriously trying to negotiate with his European friends, e.g. Bredow, he was still involved with George Liszicasz and Alexander Shereshevsky back in Vancouver. He was starting to get good effects on a fairly consistent basis. He wrote me in December that the "...device works without me as group [Liszicasz and Shereshevsky] fired it up – they produced...movements of heavy objects." He later confided that he was just told that by Shereshevsky (but see Jan 21, 1989 incident). When John did the tuning: "...I produced in their presence... a 1000 lb transformer half lifted [off] its base, nails, nails moving around nails, exploding tools curling up... There was...a grey-coloured cloud that vanished into the ceiling – pulled nails out of wall – pushed them into wall – odd." Evidently at that time two 25,000 volt 500 joule 80 lb capacitors "blew up" which explosion may have been noted in an article in the Vancouver Sun newspaper on Feb 28, 1990. According to a letter to me from Feb 20 1990, John made the now-famous series of videos showing, among other effects, the "levitating cannonball", in late 1988 and early 1989.

Somewhat wistfully, John laments "In some ways I wish I was back with the old gang [i.e. Pharos]".

1989: PCBs and Environment Canada

In the early part of the year, John was wrestling with George Liszicasz and Alexander Shereshevsky who were insisting on more effects on demand. As John was not able to produce on demand, George and Alexander were becoming increasingly annoyed. They tried to lock John out of the laboratory they had set up for him at 398 E. 13th St. in Vancouver and deny him access to his own equipment. Whether he had signed over the rights to his equipment to them is not known. Finally John served Axon General Systems, in the persons of Liszicasz and Shereshevsky with a writ. The resulting affidavit taken by Yin Gazda from the B.C. Supreme Court dated Jan 31, 1989 states that the court allowed John free access to his equipment and to take possession of it. It also forbade the defendants (Liszicasz and Shereshevsky) from disposing or transferring the equipment in advance of a trial that was to take place.

The writ and the impending trial were the result of a previous altercation with Liszicasz and Shereshevsky. On Jan 21 John and Yin Gazda were removing equipment from the lab when Liszicasz and Shereshevsky arrived with the police to tell John that he was no longer president of Axon General. They had also instructed the police to prevent John from removing equipment according to certain sections of the company's bylaws. Yin quoted Liszicasz who said outside the lab "He can have all the equipment but not now...He doesn't need the machine...He can do it without the machine. He screwed us. He knew he doesn't need the machine – he was upstairs. He did it there." Liszicasz and Shereshevsky believed that John was using psychokinesis (PK) to make the objects move. This may explain the reference to the device "working without me..." in the letter from Dec 1988 quoted above.

Perhaps Liszicasz and Shereshevsky thought that John had sold Axon on the need to equip a lab in return for a consistently operating machine. John's estimation is that they believed that they would eventually have an amazing machine which would work independently of John for sale to the military, industry etc. Maybe they wanted to keep the equipment for future use in lawsuits and knew John was planning to go to Europe, possibly with the equipment.

In any event, the police let John and Yin take what they had already packed in a van – John claimed it was mostly miscellaneous electronic test equipment but no major parts of the apparatus. Liszicasz and Shereshevsky then changed the locks on the lab. Yin went on "...they [L&S] refuse him the right to remove the equipment out of spite and resentment."

This episode at once solidified John's desire to leave forever Canada for Europe and release him from his contractual duties with Axon General. In a letter from Peter Kokoshinegg to John of February 22, Peter expressed his happiness that John has finally decided to come to Europe and noted the problems John was having with Liszicasz & Shereshevsky. John was not keeping his headaches to himself. The next day the British Columbia Supreme Court ruled that John could have unfettered access to lab and equipment from 10AM to 4PM (surely a difficulty for John) but no-one could remove it or otherwise dispose of it "...until further Order of this Court." John's counsel was Jack Kowarsky and counsel for Liszicasz & Shereshevsky was Brad Watson. John was not in attendance as he was already on his way to Germany. A letter to Kowarsky from John on Feb 24, written from Roland Bredow's Munich apartment, asked

Kowarsky to inquire about other Axon General affiliations, for example, another Liszicasz company called Owl Industries. Someone must have suggested to John that perhaps these other companies had not been incorporated properly, or that there might be some other inconsistency with which John could further strengthen his case against Liszicasz & Shereshevsky. This might have freed up his equipment entirely allowing him to ship it to Germany. He also asked Kowarsky to continue paying the rent on the laboratory, as Liszicasz & Shereshevsky certainly were not.

Apparently, Bill Ross was now feeling quite lonely and possibly jealous of Yin Gazda now that John had actually left, and was suspicious of Yin's motives in the whole affair. He wrote to Jack Houck inquiring as to what Jack thought of Yin. Jack wrote back to Bill on Feb. 28 describing how he invited Yin to several PK parties after being introduced to her by John. His belief was that Yin was not "concealing unacceptable motivations", i.e. not wanting to keep John in Europe for her own personal reasons. He went on "I have no reason to believe that Yin and Roland [Bredow] would be holding John against his will...I suggest we all relax and wish John a good time in Germany."

If Bill and John were or had been lovers, there is good reason why Bill would be concerned. In an interview with me on 26 Sept 2003 in New Westminster, BC, John stated that Bill Ross was bi-sexual when John knew him and Bill tried to interest John in a relationship. John claims not to have been interested, but stated: "Bill was in love with me then." According to John, Bill had recently completed a sex-change operation.

As John continued to be hosted by Bredow in Siegsdorf, Germany, he became more bitter about his recent experience back in Canada. He mentioned long letters to Major Tim Dear asking about Owl Industries. He wrote me that "I am a fugitive of Canada. Criminal Owl Industries destroyed my equipment, stole it and framed me...I cannot come to Canada as I will be thrown in jail."

The reason for this fear can be found in a subsequent letter of April 6 to one L. Hubbard from Richard Hawes, Environmental Safety Officer for British Columbia. Here, Hawes describes the landlord of the building where John had his laboratory during the Axon General days, a Mr. Sorenson, who contacted the Vancouver Fire Inspector. He was concerned about all the equipment sitting on his premises and the possibility of fire and the presence of PCBs in some of the equipment. Sorenson could have been tipped off about the PCBs by Liszicasz & Shereshevsky or else it could have been due to the explosion reported by the neighbours possibly resulting in the article in the Vancouver Sun newspaper Feb 28, 1990. Then again, it could have been Bill Ross. In a letter to me from early 1991, John stated "[It] all started with Bill Ross phone call to the police and Environment Canada."

In any event, Sorenson believed that the equipment had been abandoned. The Fire Inspector called the Industrial Waste Group, responsible for regulating and handling hazardous industrial waste. Representatives of the Fire Department, the Electrical Inspector, Police and the Industrial Waste Group visited the site and found a "bizarre collection of high voltage transformers, capacitors and meters. From the age of the equipment it was apparent that [they] could contain PCBs. In addition, some of the equipment contained radioactive material though not at dangerous levels." Also on site was Mr. Jay Raab, who said he was a friend of John's and who stated that "Mr. Hutchison was currently assembling a research lab in West Germany." Apparently John had asked Raab to arrange for the shipment of the equipment over to Germany and perhaps Sorenson had been previously contacted by Raab.

Hubbard informed Raab of the requirement to register any equipment that could contain PCBs and the documentation required for shipping this equipment. Hubbard also supplied names of contractors who could do the necessary work. Raab stated that he had only a short time to ship the equipment and was currently on vacation. It is highly unlikely that Raab was going to spend vacation time getting all this done even for a friend, especially in light of the present circumstances. Hubbard subsequently informed Sorenson that he could not scrap the equipment due to the PCB possibility. To add to the confusion, Sorenson stated that John owed him back rent and he wanted the equipment out of there as soon as possible. John's lawyer, Jack Kowarsky, must not have been maintaining the rent payments.

It is little wonder that John believed he would be jailed if he returned to Canada due to having unregistered PCBs and back rent due. The PCB problem would have been a much greater headache than the rent! George Liszicaŝz and Alexander Shereshevsky were no doubt greatly relieved that they had got out of that whole situation as they had absolved themselves of further involvement with John.

John had now been in Germany for a few months, hosted by Roland Bredow. No doubt John was feeling pressure to "perform" but his equipment was being held up in Canada and the way things were going, he would likely never see it again, let alone use it in Europe to levitate and destroy objects on demand. John was in a state. Bredow had paid for his trip and accommodation, and a space to set up the lab and was expecting John to do his "magic". He was not prepared to just let John return to Canada. The simplest way out was to establish a government conspiracy back in Canada to deflect attention from the reality of the situation.

By May, John was in Austria, being hosted by Peter Kokoshinegg. In a letter to myself and Alex, John sounds desperate: "The Germans want the technology and spent 100,000 Marks to get me here [and] persuaded me to get out of Canada never to return...Owl Industries destroyed my lab, stole things, misused the investors money and threatened to kill me...Also Owl Industries has Alex Pezarro diagrams [of the hydrocarbon detection device] and are procuring funds for the [further development of the] oil and gas device [without AP consent]." John then pleaded with me to get in touch with Alex Pezarro with whom he had not spoken in several months, hoping Alex could rescue the situation.

By now he believed that his laboratory was destroyed. He thought Elektra Briggs could help, as evidently she was consumed with the idea that the Germans had "kidnapped" John. I made a telephone call to her on July 11 per John's request. He had called her a few days prior from Munich, having returned there after some kind of "friction" between himself and Kokoshinegg. He was complaining to her about recurring bouts of agoraphobia and, according to Briggs, "...wants out of the whole European mess. Peter Kokoshinegg took him away to Austria. They [Peter and his wife] and the Bredow brothers are responsible for John's current situation. Needless to say, the lab will not be shipped to Austria or Germany, although there is a possibility that part of the lab may be saved."

Through my lectures on unconventional energy and propulsion technologies, I had come into contact with Leonard Holihan in London, an entrepreneur interested in developing new energy technologies. I had telephoned Holihan to ask him if he was able to assist John in getting back to Canada, however, no assistance was forthcoming.

More details of some of the effects John achieved were described in a letter to me from late summer. After stating "You are my scientific contact and everything fell apart when I left Pharos. My fault – stupid", he noted that he had sent the "cannonball" video originals to Elektra Briggs in August. He then described some effects not seen on that video, including the hovering of a 10 lb copper grate, the rare floating of a slab of steel and a 5/8 inch steel bolt, 2 – 3 inches long slowly melting and falling apart with no heat or lift. "This is the finest I got it."

He went on: "The latest events are East Bloc people who approached Roland [Bredow]. I have a 2 million dollar price tag...There were several raids on Peter Kokoshinegg's villa in Austria...I am here in Munich. Not much scientific contact." John thrived on scientists' interest in his work and was continually disappointed, as we were, when potential scientific contacts fell through. Notwithstanding, in a September 7 letter to John in Berlin from Dr. Amon, (see May 18, 1988 correspondence) Dr. Amon wanted to meet John in Munich with Roland Bredow. Amon was surprised that Bredow did not tell Amon of John being in Germany. He was very interested in the exact conditions that gave rise to the effect. “I suppose you are something like a ‘medium’...who has a key to higher information or energies...It will be very important to you to find out the conditions for your ‘working-time’ [i.e. best state for PK effects]”. After suggesting using the “scientific method” to investigate the Hutchison Effect, Amon states prophetically:

> “Well, there is another way, which is the way people with a special gift are going: They appear before the public, write papers and so on. They only want to be the focus of attention, without any interest [in inquiring about] the phenomena. Maybe they get some money for a certain time but afterwards they fall in a deep personal crisis. Believe me, it is very difficult to find [one’s way] out of such a crisis! I believe these special gifted people do not understand their mission in this world; that means they are born to show people new ways. A prophet never is born as a prophet. He first has to learn and live...before people accept him to be a wise man.”

Shortly thereafter, John made a brief trip to California, paid for by Yin Gazda. He visited Jack Houck in Huntington Beach, and others in New Mexico. During this time Elektra Briggs was trying to marshal support for getting John out of Europe and back to North America but not necessarily British Columbia. Whether she knew that John was already traveling to and from North America is not known.

By December, John was back in Munich meeting with scientists from the Fraunhofer Institute, evidently arranged by Bredow. Finally, John was getting some scientific attention and he seemed more upbeat. He noted that my lecture on the

Hutchison Effects at the 1988 PACE conference was outdated, as at that time I did not have access to the "cannonball" video for example. During this time John mentioned the theoretical research into Zero Point Energy by Dr. Puthoff in Austin, Texas. He sent notes from a "New Energy" meeting in Stuttgart with speakers including Bachmann, Bredow, Hilscher, etc. Hilscher seemed particularly concerned with John's problems and offered to visit him in Murnau so as to visit another free energy researcher, Eike Muller, in Switzerland. He further suggested that John try to get assistance from Les Adam who had just completed a new permanent magnet factory in Arkansas.[21]

[21] Pub. Note: Les Adam was the CEO of AZ Industries which moved from California to Arkansas at the time and whose brother now heads the company. Les Adam also gave a slideshow lecture at the First Conference on Future Energy, sponsored by IRI. Les Adam's DVD of his presentation is still available from Integrity Research Institute (IRI). Les talks about free energy, magnet motors, his company's *Magnet* magazine, and the "Meeting of the Minds" conferences that his company sponsored when it was located in California, that featured Paul Brown, Tom Valone, Eike Muller, and many others.

1990: John in Europe II; Headaches in Canada

In January I received two letters from John in Munich. John appreciated my offer to help in sorting out his situation in British Columbia and Germany, although nothing specific was decided upon. He mentioned the good results he had obtained prior to leaving for Europe: "Samples you have never seen...reports of mixed wood and metal samples tested by Siemens. I still feel Pharos...is the only group [that was seriously investigating the effect]...[these analyses] may allow for major funds but only with Pharos Technologies [emphasis JH's]". A friend of Bill Ross's, Larry Hampson, had witnessed the effects of the prior year first hand.

He wanted photos of all the samples I had to be sent to him to forward to unnamed Swiss scientists. Evidently, these scientists declared that the Hutchison Effect in the wrong hands could make the H-bomb obsolete. He had also written his Member of Parliament in Ottawa, Chuck Cook, to see if any of his laboratory still existed. John was concerned about keeping up payments on the storage of his remaining equipment. Author Jeane Manning had been apprised of John's situation and had called me for advice several times thereafter. Once again he complained about the bad treatment he received from George Liszicasz and Alexander Shereshevsky in Canada as well as from Peter Kokoshinegg in Austria who tried to get critical information on the Hutchison technology. John refused to divulge the information "So he dismissed me from Austria months ago."

He wrote hopefully: “I am on my way back to Canada – first the East Coast.” The truth was that John would not actually return to Canada until the end of 1990.

John finally realized things were getting serious back in Vancouver. He wrote from Munich to Andrew Michrowski of PACE in Ottawa that Inspector Richard Glue from the BC Ministry of Environment may charge him for unauthorized storage and transportation of PCBs upon his arrival back in the New World. He asked Andrew to contact Environment Canada and the Prime Minister to intercede on his behalf. “Things only get worse… I have no legal support. Finished I am – looks that way.”

A few weeks later John wrote to thank me for the photos and papers which he sent to a Dr. Moheim in Switzerland as well as Dr. Karl Walters of the World Research Foundation in Los Angeles. Moheim’s comments were positive but he said that the world was not ready for such a technology.

“I had some bad encounters by groups unknown – threats to me – telegram type letters plus Kristofsky (?) put a 2 million dollar price tag on my head. The telegram letters are...death threats if I do not cooperate. I ignored them” Apparently Dr. Panos Pappas had warned John about Kristofsky. I never found out who this person was. John also phoned Leonard Holihan who told him of the Prince of Liechtenstein, Hans-Adam, who had an interest in unusual technology. John did in fact contact Prince Hans-Adam. However, “All this delayed my departure to Canada until my ticket is no longer any good.”

Elektra Briggs had the original of the “cannonball” video. “I mailed it to her.” John wrote. He also noted that: “I had a large amount of data - all this data was stolen by GL & AS [Liszicasz & Shereshevsky] plus they took a video and a lab notebook.” Apparently a person called “Brent” had taken part in the “cannonball” experiments in early 1989 and then took some large samples to Europe in 1989, one of which was a 3” x 3” block of steel 8 kg in weight which exploded from the inside out like the aluminum samples. John never saw him or the samples again. More samples had been given to Mr. Kovaks who evidently represented Boeing in Seattle, and who was a friend of Liszicasz.

In Europe, "Many people wanted me to show how the device worked but I did not say anything as I feel Pharos is still alive and well." This was no doubt the cause of the Europeans' frustrations with John. "As you know, I am as 'one' with such a system. I feel the research is very vital now! [emphasis JH's]...I can only trust you and the proper group – Tom Bearden, John Alexander, Alexis [Pezarro]. My worst mistake was when I left Pharos but I was not 100 percent in the head so to speak." Regarding his old friend Roland Bredow: "I would not contact Bredow at all...He got involved with several types – one kidnapped him, also broke into his apartment."

The Vancouver Sun newspaper ran a story by Glenn Bohn, environmental reporter, on February 28 entitled "Ministry secretly builds PCB storage site in Surrey". The article claimed that the BC Environment Ministry had just recently built new PCB storage facility without getting the necessary hazardous waste storage permit. Apparently they would have had to have given it to themselves but this would have necessitated prior public hearings which would have taken too long. The article went on:

> "The environment ministry had the PCB storage area set up last summer after the discovery of a laboratory in east Vancouver in March [1989]. The lab was a large room full of high-voltage electrical equipment – some of which was laden with polychlorinated biphenyls...Eleven barrels of toxic PCBs... came from [the] lab...Rick Hawes, a BC environmental safety officer...said...that there had once been an explosion. 'We felt it simply had to be removed and cleaned up.' Authorities had telephone calls from people who claimed that the 'inventor' was being held against his will in Eastern Europe: they heard claims that a rival company was trying to steal the invention."

This whole affair obviously caused a lot of embarrassment in local government circles and ill will towards John.

In response to John's initial contact via Leonard Holihan, Prince Hans-Adam wrote a letter in reply dated March 7 and noted having seen a video which I had shown Prince Hans-Adam in 1989 in an attempt to assist John. The Prince stated: "The problem I see is that we do not know if the effect is produced by the complicated machinery or an extraordinary parapsychological talent you personally have. To answer this question one would have to start a very serious research programme... I think that in the future we might spend some time and money to research the "Hutchison Effect"." John responded in a letter thanking him for his interest and looking forward to a possible meeting.

John traveled to Austria for a month in April but he complained "There is not much for me to do here but receive bad news. This compounds a melancholy state I am in so my health is not at its best...In this world of events – odd things – I need your contact to keep my spirits up...I feel you, Alexis and others we know are the only ones to take a serious look." However, while in Austria, he rid himself of an old habit: valium. Apparently Margareta Kokoshinegg had started John on a new health regimen in 1989 which eventually led to his giving up valium and several other dependencies. On another bright note, John received a telephone call from Randy Gott of Gott Industries, Vancouver, who said that he would take care of the remaining boxes of John's equipment. Several boxes of John's gun collection and personal effects still needed storage "...before All Cargo Express of Vancouver will auction it all off." Apparently he could not store the boxes at Bill Ross's "...for personal reasons."

During most of John's visit to Europe, Bill Ross, Elektra Briggs and Jeane Manning were in touch with me trying to find ways to get John away from his European "kidnappers", to use Elektra Briggs' term. In contrast to their expressions of grave concern, John himself seemed to waffle between a quiet desperation and a begrudging acceptance of his current state: he wrote: “George, all is OK. Billie Ross may try to phone you or my friend Elektra Briggs. But I mentioned to him I have no wishes to ever return to B.C.” and later in a letter of May 21: “I am helpless here, also I have no plane fare [to return to North America].”

However, by late 1990, John had made his way back to Canada, apparently disgruntled with how things were (not) progressing in Europe and a desire to straighten out his affairs in Canada.

1991: The Prince of Liechtenstein and PACE

John was now staying at 145 SE Marine Drive in Vancouver. In a January letter, he attached an invoice from the Canadian Department of External Affairs which evidently had loaned John $145 on July 24, 1990 in Bonn, Germany to assist him in getting his passport in order for the eventual return to Canada. I paid the outstanding invoice as John had returned to Canada virtually broke.

He further described how he had been able to retain a few "important pieces" of the original lab before it was closed down, but "most of the high voltage stuff is gone." He went on: "I was told by word of mouth...all points to the Government not wanting me to have it [the lab] and used Environment Canada as the tool." Here is the first written indication that John was starting to think that there was a concerted effort, a conspiracy on the part of the government, to destroy his lab. John believed it started with Bill Ross telephoning the police and Environment Canada and "squealing" on him and continued with Elektra Briggs and Ross compounding stories of intrigue. Not surprisingly, one of those apparently spreading this conspiracy rumour was Alexander Shereshevsky.

John discussed some simple experiments at a small lab he had set up at his sister Margo's garage on Dublin St. "To my surprise I got some results with dual signal generators and electrostatics. I would safely say it is a form of contamination I got from the large machine…I would like your advice." This was reminiscent of the late Rudolf Zinsser's and Jacques Benveniste's experiments where unusual effects remained associated with certain equipment (or water in Zinsser's and Benveniste's case) for long periods of time after the power was turned off. He also mentioned sending the original "cannonball" video to Elektra Briggs and a copy to Andrew Michrowski of PACE in Ottawa, plus 200 odd documents and 2 metal samples. Evidently Yin Gazda was now keen on meeting Tom Bearden in anticipation of a possible movie about the paranormal featuring John.

Sounding much more upbeat, John wrote "I have some good solid plans and have been busy at the lab" but wanted to sell some of his gun collection so as to get back to Germany. John just couldn't settle down. Pressing on with his experiments, he was determined to try "...one vacuum tube Tesla coil [as in his early lab experiments] one static unit, one small nuclear source with copper mass units and geometric forms. Now I would send out 250 kHz [to] 12 gHz…I did this in 1988 at the 13th St lab." He then described attempts to make a microwave-based "energy machine" using waveguide, radium chloride and "tiny germanium crystals" and reported 5 volts at 300 milliamps (mA). Evidently, some groups in Europe were still intrigued enough to want John back to demonstrate his new energy machines.

February saw the first concerted effort by a free energy group to exert some control over the Hutchison Effect. John needed money to finance further experimentation on the energy devices he was envisioning and so naturally canvassed everyone he could think of for assistance upon his return from Europe. Evidently, his acquaintances in North America were keen to help him become established back home in order to avoid the temptations of Europe. He had already sent a copy of the Mar 7, 1990 letter he received from Prince Hans-Adam of Liechtenstein to Andrew Michrowski of PACE concerning the Prince's previous interest in the effect. Michrowski took it upon himself to try to convince the Prince to renew his interest and fund John's work (through PACE, of course). Andrew saw clearly that this was a golden opportunity to raise the status of PACE worldwide if it could be seen to be a fund-raiser and project manager of a "technology" with as far-reaching consequences as the Hutchison Effect.

Excerpts from Andrew's letter to Prince Hans-Adam of February 4th are quoted below:

> "Our association's network has been stewarding and facilitating the experimental work of John Hutchison since the late 1970s."
>
> "George Hathaway, while initiating monitoring of the "Hutchison Effect", was then Vice-President of the Association. Over the years, other qualified expert members of our association have become involved this pioneering endeavour."
>
> "Specifically, our association considers the 'Hutchison Effect' to be the result of the interplay of physical variables and not the result of some "extraordinary parapsychological event... Therefore we suggest that you do not consider embarking [sic] 'a very serious research programme', only to check whether the 'Hutchison Effect' is merely a personal rather than an independently replicable series of phenomena."
>
> "Surely the benefits of scalar electromagnetics, including those developed by John Hutchison – including for the healing arts [an area of little interest to the Prince at the time] - merit exploitation and not just academic, exploratory research."

This letter is typical of the many misguided attempts by marginal players in the Hutchison saga to push their own agendas and thereby garner a certain fame for themselves while attempting to assist John in his endeavours. Here, Andrew implies that PACE had been a prime driving force in John's experimental work since the 1970s. This was a complete fabrication. While PACE did publish my paper in their 1988 Conference proceedings[22] and accepted various small articles for their newsletter, they were in no way involved in the experimentation. Andrew tried to downplay Pharos' involvement while boosting his own in the Prince's eyes. I was never a Vice-President of PACE nor was I ever an officer of the organization. Other "qualified" members of PACE were involved in trying to understand, from a distance, the phenomena (e.g. Tom Bearden), but no PACE member was intimately involved apart from myself and Alex. Andrew made a fatal blunder in assuming that the Prince was only interested in determining the psychotronic aspects of the Hutchison Effect.

Not only did Andrew attempt to pre-empt the Prince on the psychotronic issue, he also tried to shame the Prince into supporting a wider development ("exploitation") effort of areas of interest to PACE. This aggressive and condescending tone contributed to the withdrawal of the Prince's interest in supporting John through PACE and indicated to the Prince to be extremely wary of subsequent attempts by others to request funding and offers to "manage" John's research (for a small fee, of course). The Prince did not want to be forced to make deals with "managers" who had no experience with John.

Clearly the Prince did not fall for this ill-considered overture. In a letter to John of Feb. 22, the Prince thanked John for his recent papers and letters and respectfully declined to fund the research: "Your research is certainly very interesting and I hope that you will be successful in finding further support ...I hope that you will understand if I do not support your research project." This is a kind way of stating he did not want to get involved in a project with so many potential

---

[22] Pub. Note: Third International Symposium on Non-Conventional Energy, held in Ottawa, Ontario in 1988. Proceedings available from PACE.

problems and pitfalls (3 failed demonstrations, inventor variously in Europe and North America, potential problems with government agencies, bad blood between inventor and previous funders (Axon), many other individuals and groups trying to get involved, etc.). The possibility that the effect was psi-related and that much more pure research was necessary was not an issue in turning down John's request.

John was of course disappointed with the Prince's response but was also concerned about the tone of Andrew Michrowski's letter. But he did not give up. On March 14, he sent another letter to the Prince stating that only I (George Hathaway) would administer the research if funded by the Prince. Interestingly, he also stated: "Part of the device is parapsychological – these are mild effects without the equipment...with the equipment the effects are many orders of magnitude stronger." Unfortunately, the Prince had now committed himself to other projects and was not able to respond positively to this request either.

Later in March, he wrote to me that: "I do know that I played a part [in the effect] but I feel anybody can...The effect, I feel, is so close to being understood now, even if it is PK...I have studied Jack Houck's report...please take it seriously."

Coincidentally, John received a letter in late Feb from Jack Houck in California. He was now living at his sister's house on Dublin St. after being forced out of the Marine Drive location by a tip-off to Owl Industries. Jack related:

> "Your recent letter to me suggests you are experiencing more paranormal phenomena than the 'normal' people do."
>
> "Your mind goes out and coheres the local available energy which then creates a force which attempts to achieve the goal [e.g. levitation or low temp melting]"

> "Creating a peak emotional event at the time you want the phenomena event to happen also seems to be an important ingredient."

Again, he wished John good luck with his researches.

After another royal rejection, this time from Austrian Prince Schwartzenberg, John was becoming concerned that he may not get enough funding to return with what remained of his laboratory to Europe. He also desperately needed a place to store his remaining equipment since leaving the Marine Drive location as his sister needed room in her garage. John suggested that maybe I could pay to ship his equipment to my laboratory in Toronto for storage and possible use. I faxed him requesting information on the number of skids he had, total shipping weight, declaration of dangerous goods (e.g. radioactive materials, PCBs), etc. I needed to know this information before my shipping company would touch it. John never provided the information.

Meanwhile, John was relating to me his experiences in Europe. He first recalled how at the 13th St. laboratory, the best activity in 1989 was 5 events per hour. The effect frequency dropped to 1 per day in Germany where he had the electrostatic machine and the "projector" [?] plus dual signal generators at 475 MHz and 7 MHz. In Austria the effects were down to 1 per week but evidently he did witness a cardboard box fly off the table. John ascribes the effects in Germany and Austria to "...the contamination of working with the LADS over the years [emphasis JH's]." Recall John's earlier concern about contamination.

In September, John received a letter from John Alexander after repeated requests from John to send a copy of the INSCOM demonstration report and videos. John Alexander reported:

> "As I suspected, the Los Alamos paper addressing the observation of the experiment conducted in Vancouver

no longer exists. The experiment was conducted eight years ago in 1983 and those files have long since been routinely destroyed."

"...John Rink...was one of the observers...His recollection and mine about the report are the same; the report was extremely negative...The report would only have served as very prejudicial against you and your work."

"John...no results were observed by me or the team."

1992: Conspiracy

Both Alex and I had fallen out of touch with John's peregrinations for much of 1992. However, John did keep me informed of his continued push for the INSCOM report in spite of the direct denial of its existence from John Alexander. He was under increasing pressure from "concerned individuals" who were slowly convincing him that the US government was involved in a great conspiracy to withhold the INSCOM non-demonstration report for its own nefarious purposes. He contacted the CIA but they said they couldn't help.

He continued to do small experiments in the Dublin St. garage but was unsuccessful in repeating any of the effects from the 1980s. His mind was increasingly occupied by his oven-baked energy cells, one of which he claimed was able to produce 3-4 volts at 400 mA. He was also tinkering with solar flux measurement, extremely low-frequency radio, earthquake precursors etc.

In April, his love, Yin Gazda, said goodbye only to return at the end of the year. She stayed with him until 1994 and then finally went back to Hollywood. John applied to emigrate to Austria, but nothing came of the attempt.

Alex finally went to visit John in November, the first time they had seen each other in years. Evidently they "Had a good day talking of the days we had together and how impossible I was in those days." He wrote me that he had found the original of the "cannonball" video from the 1988 and 1989 time.

1993: Dr. Hal Puthoff

John was now getting farther and farther away from the ability to reproduce the famous effects of the 1980s. More and more international media were finding out about the Canadian "inventor of anti-gravity" and sending film crews to interview him for various television shows and films on the paranormal. He was being asked to make more of his "Dirt Cheap – Shake and Bake-Crystal Converter" energy cells for demonstration and sale.

One prominent supporter involved in creating the Hutchison media persona was a Japanese businessman, Mr. Hiroshi Yamabe. John's first mention of Mr. Yamabe was in a January letter to me from John, still living at his sister's house on Dublin St. He mentions Mr. Yamabe and a Mr. Yokoyama of the Japanese magazine "Space Power" having been given early copies of the "cannonball" video. John also sold a piece of his equipment, a "space gun" to Yamabe.

John also summed up other video interviews:

- BCTV CTV "Newshour" demonstration 8 minutes 1984
- CKVU (Vancouver?) TV demonstration 5 minutes 1985

- CBC news story 5 minutes 1987 no demonstration but interview with Alex Pezarro & John
- Yin Gazda's movie "Miracles of the Unknown" (unknown release date) had a segment on John

On May 18th, I had a lengthy telephone conversation with John in which we discussed the 1989 "cannonball" video, the video of the most interesting Hutchison Effects. I asked him whether he had made a sketch of the 1988 setup. He said he had sent one to Charles Yost of the publication "Electric Spacecraft Journal" to publish (see Electric Spacecraft Journal #4, Oct/Nov/Dec 1991 pg 16).[23] Regarding the numerous burn spots on a plywood board used as a base for some of the samples, John said he didn't recall precisely but did report having spontaneous combustion of the wood on occasion, a phenomena I personally witnessed in the bare concrete floor during one of my visits prior to the INSCOM demonstration. During the filming, John picked up readily-available "stuff" and threw it into the field from time to time. As to where the samples landed: some flew at the camera and around in a loop and then shot off to one side but most hit the ceiling and shot off to one side.

I asked what was the "lumpy jelly" in the bowls that seemed to boil. It was a mixture of ice and water plus some chemicals. The ice melted during the filming. The "flashlight" effects were caused by John playing with a concave mirror for fun. The "cannonball" was a cast iron 8" diameter milling ball. It took about ½ hour for the last bar in the film to break up.

"All [the equipment] was set up and let run wild all day." John walked away from and around active area without adjusting anything during the filming. All the filming was done when Owl Industries (George Liszicasz and Alexander Shereshevsky) were away but evidently they filmed lots of

---

[23] Pub. Note: Back Issues of *Electric Spacecraft Journal* are available from http://www.electricspacecraft.com/bissues.htm (Issue #4 is on "The Hutchison Effect.")

activity on other occasions as well while John was present. A friend named Brent (?) was present from time to time. The video camera was usually 8 – 12 feet from active area and moving all the time because it was a heavy Sony Vu-matic camera with no tripod and John had to put it down periodically.

During the conversation, John stated "There were psychokinetic (PK) events in Germany [about which] I wrote to Jack Houck." John believed there was PK involved. "I must be highly excited to achieve these results or suffering from lack of sleep."

From a later fax, John related that most tests during this period were performed using household (120 VAC) mains current at about 1200 watts but occasionally he would insert a piece of additional equipment bringing the maximum power draw to about 1800 watts.

As for the future: "I would really have to think hard about doing it again."

In early June, I sent the outline of a proposal to Prince Hans-Adam Liechtenstein to once again try to assist John in setting up his lift and disruption experiments. In a letter to John of June 9, the Prince thanked John for his letters and Yin Gazda's video. He went on to state: "I am very happy about the progress you have made and I discussed with George Hathaway how we should proceed from now on." On July 22, 1993, the Prince approved the proposal in general but insisted that I be the project manager, not one of John's many self-appointed "handlers". He also stressed the need to keep his involvement completely confidential and keep the media at bay so that John could concentrate on the research.

Just prior to this, Dr. Hal Puthoff and I visited John to handle some of the actual samples from his numerous videos and also discuss his various energy devices. Dr. Puthoff was duly impressed, especially concerning the samples in which foreign materials e.g. a knife blade, copper pennies or wood slivers, were found embedded in aluminum blocks without evidence of heating. John sent a fax to Dr. Puthoff in late June from Apt 306, 731 5th Ave. New Westminster, thanking Dr.

Puthoff for his visit and the scientific papers Dr. Puthoff had provided him. "I am much enlightened by your papers, the Casimir effect haunts me...The capacitors I used [for early lift experiments] were NCR 500 joule low inductance 25,000 VDC Pyranol [i.e. PCB] and 1.6 mfd."

Around this time, I prepared a 3 hour video containing all the essential parts of the "Hutchison Affair" that seemed important, including video segments with commentary, pictures of samples, electron micrographs, "experts" pontificating on how it was all done and a historical summary, etc. This was done primarily to assist John in raising funds to further his research as I sent him the originals to enable him to make copies for sale. In a mid-July letter, John thanked me for the video and stated "Your scientific observations are OK and on target." He hoped I could develop a reasonable theory of what was happening. In that, I have so far failed.

At that time, to our great sadness, our friend and colleague, Alex Pezarro died of a sudden heart attack just as he and John were renewing their friendship. Almost coincidentally John's father died. At about this time as well, Dr. Kokoshinegg died in Austria. He mourned Alex's passing as well as his own father's: "My dad and I were worlds apart yet towards the end Yin [Gazda] made it possible for me to see him in a different light... I feel I am not yet recovered from these two powerful blows in my life."

In a letter to me dated July 27th, John acknowledged receipt of my proposal sent July 17 and stated: "All the points you mentioned sound very pleasing to me...The people we can trust...are the ones we know, the professionals...I totally understand...about secrecy." Notwithstanding this concurrence, he did wish to maintain his connections to the media outside the laboratory: the various publications, lectures, movies, etc.

In addition, he mentioned sending me a black and white video of the 1986 setup and bemoans sending the original of another from 1987 to Elektra Briggs. It was taken by a friend named Don Muses. In a later correspondence, John stated that the Muses video was taken at the 560 Cambie St. laboratory at the office of a company called Car-Check of Canada. He later did a voice-over for that silent Muses video.

While contemplating whether to agree to the terms of the proposal involving Prince Hans-Adam, John was courting other possible investors, such as the RIA Trade group in Vancouver who had become interested in his work a few months prior. When I pointed out this potential conflict, John agreed that there was a problem but still wished to pursue his free energy experiments and turn over the manufacturing to others, e.g. Pierre Sinclair or Roland Bredow while plowing the expected royalties back into LADS research. He mused about taking the Hutchison Effect into other areas such as medicine, "…as Alexis once told me – it is a Pandora's box." Perhaps he was thinking of using himself as a research subject. He had applied for provincial medical disability insurance coverage upon his arrival back in Canada. In an August letter, he stated: "The only disability I have is really in my own mind, meaning that the agoraphobic or panic disorder is a biological, psychological thing but far removed since 1988… As I mentioned to you and Dr. Puthoff,[24] I am open to anything including brain scans, EEG or whatever if we suspect a psychotronic factor."[25] It is interesting to note that the last major Hutchison Effects were filmed around this time.

Here he mentions for the first time his nascent interest in "life extension research": "My goal is to get off of such a situation [i.e. get off drugs]… I am having some success with diet, vitamins, minerals, amino acids, enzymes." He also received an inheritance from his father's estate of some $120,000 with which he and Yin were planning a trip to Austria in September.

---

[24] See details about Dr. Puthoff in p. 26 footnote – Pub. Note

[25] Pub. Note: "psychotronics" is a term coined after Czech researchers in the 1970s to indicate a mind-matter connection achieved through special electronic equipment. IRI also publishes two psychotronics books, originally edited from the best papers from three decades of USPA conferences, called *Energetic Processes*, Volume I & II, also available on Amazon.com.

After his return from Austria, I again offered John the opportunity to come to Toronto to perform experiments. John responded "I understand your offer and look forward to how you wish to proceed, as one almost has to feel the machines when working with them [emphasis JH's]." However, he was fielding offers from around the world by this time – primarily from Japan and Germany. There were offers to write a book from a David Spines and Mr. Yokoyama which never fully materialized. This activity occupied much of his attention: "Hopefully I can soon get my energy back...and lend my support to the group of yours." All this media attention eventually killed any plans we had with Prince Hans-Adam.

1994: John in Japan; Brian O'Leary's Statue

The New Year saw John living at 731 5th Ave., New Westminster. He wanted me to send him some small samples of iron from a large steel bar that had crumbled at one end. Alex Pezarro had sent me the samples for analysis in the early 1980s. Evidently he wanted to observe the surfaces by Scanning Electron Microscopy even though I had already published the SEM photos in the 1988 PACE conference proceedings. Although I never knew exactly why he wished to repeat the SEM analysis, he did state "It will be used as a reference to another odd sample that was given to me." Perhaps the other odd sample was a Siberian meteorite that he and Yin had purchased in Vienna.

In February John and Yin traveled to Santa Fe, New Mexico, and in March to Japan. According to John, the Japanese trip was very successful and in a fax of April 18, he stated: "I found a production company awaiting me asking me, besides an interview I gave, for a master quality copy of the lab experiments on video and 8 mm film." He went on to demand that I provide him with master copies of all film and video in my possession as well as all lab analyses on the samples. His tone was brusque: “Please do not hesitate to provide me with all these documents, since too much valuable time has passed.” In May I sent him a package containing the original master of the 3 hour video I had made for him plus copies of the 8 mm film he and Alex had taken as well as copies of all SEM, XRF & acceleration plots, all of which had been provided already to him via Alex Pezarro years before. This was a clear indication to me the degree to which the media held John in its thrall.

In addition, John firmly requested the large (14” long) steel bar itself which was the source of the small samples already sent to him a few months before. This was done on Jun 22. Prior to that, John and Yin attended a conference in Denver in May at which I also presented a paper.

In August he again asked for the master copy of my 3 hour video which I had already sent some months prior. It is likely that he had forwarded it to one of his new-found media fiends and not made a copy for himself. I reminded him that I had already sent him the original 2-tape master from which I made Charles Yost’s 1-tape master. I had previously given this to Yost so he could make duplicates for sale with the proceeds going only to John.

By November, John was living at 727 5th Ave., New Westminster, Apt 305. To quote from a fax of Nov 26:

> “I have had some major events that have concerned me a bit. I could have been contaminated by all those fields. Since 1989 I have had PK events, more dramatic in the last year. One of the most powerful was before 3 witnesses, one of them a scientist Brian O’Leary[26] and his wife and Yin. I happened to supposedly melt down a statue made of pewter. For two years this large statue, maybe a few

---

[26] Pub. Note: The late Dr. Brian O’Leary, physicist, was also a retired NASA astronaut who authored books on free energy, most notably, *Miracle in the Void* and *The Energy Solution Revolution* .

pounds, sat on an old wood stove that would always be lit. I sat down that evening in a high state of feeling [emphasis JH's] and thus the statue fell apart."

Concerning this event, he later (Feb 1995) wrote "The event at Brian O'Leary's home of the metal statue falling apart into globs in front of his wife and Yin... So I speculate a possible contamination on me with working with the energy."

The November fax went on to describe other events such as "computers, stores, banks go down as my turn comes to the wicket, electrical devices...go haywire." He notes that the only new factor in his life is taking large amounts of L-arginine, L-ornithine and many different vitamins, minerals and enzymes in his life extension quest.

1995: More "Crystal Energy Cells"

As time progressed, John focused his attention more on his energy cells and media appearances than researching the lift and disruption phenomena. Early in 1995 he laments that although he tried to bring back the major movements of material he was only able to achieve "very minor movements at random". The last major effect he noted was the breakup of O'Leary's statue. So he pressed on with his energy generating schemes, variously called the "crystal energy converters", "dirt-cheap" or "shake and bake" devices. As John described to me, the latter two types consisted of packing a random mixture of various minerals found in scrap yards and other locations into metallic cylinders with a variety of types of central electrode embedded in the middle, much like a conventional dry cell battery. He would concoct several of these at one time and literally bake them in his kitchen oven until the mass solidified. Some of them actually produced a measurable current for varying lengths of time. Other forms of "crystal energy cells" relied on external stimulation of piezoelectric cylinders typically of barium titanate in some configuration claimed to produce excess energy.

He wrote that he had completed a unit comprising 3 large barium titanate cylinders weighing 30 lb and producing 1 – 3 volts at 3 amps in pulses as measured though a 10 amp meter, essentially a short circuit. He did not report on the duty cycle to enable one to estimate the average power produced. This unit he was planning to take to Japan for a demonstration. Apparently he later broke this unit apart and rebuilt it as a 1 volt unit powering a tiny fan. Another device was claimed to have an output at 300-1000 volts but at milliamps.

In a fax from February 3, John described additional details about the so-called crystal energy unit: "…no moving parts or antennas or primer voltage. The unit collects energy from fine point contact on crystal that is in a tube with a pressure tuning control…The crystalline interfaces or ionic bonds are where to look in metallic crystals [for energy extraction]."

Hal Puthoff also corresponded with John from time to time concerning the energy devices which Hal had recently witnessed operating. He congratulated John for his improvements to the earlier device which Hal and I witnessed several months prior. Hal also described a possible approach to energy conversion from the vacuum zero point fluctuation field of quantum physics. This involved consideration of Casimir effects at the myriad boundaries of the dissimilar materials contained in John's energy cells. Hal even suggested a collaboration whereby Hal would make long-term energy measurements on the device and perhaps receive some crystalline material to duplicate the effect. Nothing came of this suggestion.

Perhaps it was this interaction that led John to start associating the crystal energy converters with zero point energy. After returning from Japan, John stated that the Japanese were calling the device a Zero Point Energy Machine. The likelihood that the energy production has anything to do with zero point fluctuations is remote in the extreme.

The View from 2009

During all his adventures, John never lost his curiosity and playful approach to life. He has survived numerous setbacks that would have caused a lesser person to switch career paths long ago. Surprisingly he has made far more friends and believers than disbelievers. Although the wider scientific community as a whole is likely to completely disregard the Hutchison Effect as totally spurious, when confronted on an individual basis, most scientists consider the effects intriguing.

Although nowadays John takes pains to play down the possible psychokinetic aspects, no-one I am aware of can provide any other theory that explains the totality of the phenomena, assuming there is no fakery involved. It should be clear that during the period covered in this book, John and others seriously entertained the possibility of mind-machine interaction whereby the assemblage of equipment acted as a psychokinetic amplifier of John's own innate abilities. This bears more than casual scrutiny for several reasons.

First, discussions and publications about anomalous mind-matter interactions are becoming more commonplace in the scientific literature. Although the bulk of the reported experiments rely on delicate mechanical or electronic systems which incorporate or exhibit random outcomes, there does not appear to be a fundamental limit to the ultimate strength of these effects.

It is tempting to try to make a strong correlation between John's mental state and the frequency of the activity. I have not investigated this aspect of the phenomena in detail but I would not completely discount the likelihood that there may be a small correspondence between, say, the failed major demonstrations and John's emotional life.

The Hutchison apparatus has continually changed in both number and type of components as well as the way they are interconnected. Over time, John would add or subtract various pieces of apparatus that he typically hand made. The earliest constructions such as those put together by Alex and me were relatively simple affairs but towards the early 1990s the individual pieces of equipment became larger and there were more of them. Apparently the recent (ca 2008) demonstrations to various film crews used a much fewer number of components, as did the attempts in Europe in the mid-1990s.

Also it is noteworthy that during our association with John, he had to be physically present for any activity to occur even if we, Alex and myself, had set up the apparatus ourselves.

As will be evident from Part II of this book, the main electromagnetic field-producing devices, the Tesla coils, were not supplied with power in the way we would normally understand it. My crude field readings in the 1980s registered no unusually large electromagnetic fields near the active area or even next to the main Tesla coil. It is painfully clear that there is no conventional physics theory that can explain the movements and fragmentation I personally witnessed.

This continual alteration to the device is also one of the reasons that the Hutchison Effect is so difficult to scientifically investigate. Since there is not one single configuration, it could be argued that an almost arbitrary configuration might result in various, if not all, of the phenomena.

Many of the videos captured by John and now posted in profusion on the internet show effects that could have been faked, some more easily than others. I cannot comment on the likelihood of fakery in the years after Alex Pezarro died. However, having followed the free energy movement since 1979, I have seen many examples of a pathology particular to such inventors. After initial actual or perceived success with an invention, the inventor is pressured by his/her backers or acolytes to continue to make the invention better, stronger, faster, more repeatable etc. If the inventor is unable to repeat the initial success, this pressure often becomes unbearable and the inventor resorts to a bit of trickery to buy time. Life is made more difficult when the initial discovery is evanescent. This is emphatically not an accusation or designed to impugn John's achievements, but rather as a general response to those who would pillory such inventors without probing into the genesis of the invention. It is within the realm of possibility that Mary and Filippo Galluppi, Alex Pezarro and I were duped during our witnessing of the phenomenon but highly unlikely. It is also possible that Alex, Mel Winfield and many other early witnesses had been duped during his many early private demonstrations and experiments, but highly unlikely. Why anyone would attempt some kind of subterfuge during demonstrations of such importance as those set up by Pharos is difficult to imagine.

The conclusion to which I am forced to admit is that there was and still possibly is a highly anomalous phenomenon associated with John Hutchison that conventional physics cannot yet address. Whether we will find the answer as a result of experimentation involving John and his apparatus is not known but seems to diminish in likelihood as time goes by. This is a shame.

PART II: The Circuit Diagrams

Several technical descriptions of varying degrees of specificity have been published[27] as well as presented on various websites[28]. Therefore, I will not repeat these in detail here except to note that they contain sketches of the physical layout and block circuit diagram for the INSCOM demonstration as well as some spectrum analyzer and oscilloscope photos of the electric and magnetic field readings. They also contain photos, scanning electron micrographs and elemental analyses of some metal samples subjected to the effect. A few photos of some metal samples are included in this book for reference. Readers interested in the dimensions of some of the major components are directed to a useful Hutchison compendium published by the Planetary Association for Clean Energy[29].

---

[27] For example, see Hathaway, G., *The Hutchison Effect – A Lift and Disruption System*, A. Michrowski, ed. The Third International New Energy Technology Symposium, June 1988, available from the Planetary Association for Clean Energy, 100 Bronson Ave, Suite 1001, Ottawa, Canada K1R 6G8, 1990 and Electric Spacecraft Journal, Issue # 4, Oct/Nov/Dec 1992

[28] For example, see www.americanantigravity.com

[29] Calante, P., Michrowski, A. (Eds) "The Hutchison File", Planetary Association for Clean Energy, 1996

Of primary interest here is a more detailed description of the various pieces of apparatus and how they were interconnected during my involvement with John. According to John, the physical placement of the various transformers, Tesla coils, electrostatic machine, etc. were critical to the eventual manifestation of the effect. Therefore I am including photos of the physical space (see Part III) and placement of the equipment. A primary objective of this presentation is to demonstrate that a variety of configurations of various equipment has been used by John over the years and that, apart from the electrostatic machine and Tesla coils, no particular equipment was vital. I am not aware of the various configurations John uses at present, however.

John divided the apparatus into three main sections: "[electro]static", "RF" (radio frequency) and "substation", i.e. power supplies. The first section consisted of the van de Graaff electrostatic machine and various other pieces connected to it in various ways. The RF (radio frequency) section's principal components were large hand-made Tesla coils, more correctly called Tesla transformers. In the earliest tests, a small radio transmitter accompanied the large Tesla coil but in later tests, a smaller vacuum-tube driven Tesla coil and a double-ended "dumbbell" Tesla coil were used, but sometimes no other RF source than the large Tesla coil. A large jumble of additional components was variously used including high-voltage capacitors, spark-gaps, inductors and coils of various types and home-made bits and pieces. Power for the entire apparatus came from either one or two common 110 VAC wall plugs plugged into common wall sockets. These supplied mains power for the high-voltage transformers and other high-voltage power supplies, as well as the small Tesla coil and van de Graaff electrostatic machine. In addition, John usually put a weak radioactive source in a metal tube somewhere near the active area.

John's method of interconnecting these various pieces of equipment was simply to string low-voltage insulated wire from one terminal to another. This hook-up wire was typically kept apart by hanging it from strings fastened to the ceiling. There was actually a reason why this was done instead of properly routing the wires from device to device. That was because he continually moved the devices to slightly different positions during the tuning phase, and usually between experiments, in order to maximize the effects.

The three circuit diagrams shown here are my hand-drawn electrical schematics from the apparatus configurations which produced either lift or material disruption or both. Figure 1 is from the Murphy's basement. This laboratory was so crowded with components related or not to the experimentation that all photographs of the apparatus had to be taken at close range. Therefore I have not included photos of the early laboratory. The INSCOM tests were in a more spacious room and photographs of that series of tests are included in Part III of this book. These photos will give the reader some sense of the component size and placement in relation to the circuit diagrams.

Figure 3 from July, 1983 shows the circuit after Alex and I had re-constructed the apparatus from its state shown in Figure 2. In preparation for the INSCOM demonstration, we constructed the apparatus according to Figure 2 in the new location without John's assistance. When we only achieved minor effects, attributable to electrostatics, John rearranged the apparatus to that shown in Figure 3 and produced more consistent and spectacular results. He added many new components including a large flat spiral coil which he mounted on a wall near the rest of the apparatus.

In the circuit diagrams each major component is numbered. The following legend will help the reader identify them and allow a correspondence to be made to various components shown in the photos in Part III. It is assumed that the reader has some familiarity with schematic diagrams. Several component numbers have been omitted for clarity.

The Hutchison Circuit Components

Component Number	Description
1.	10 kilovolt (kV) 60 milliamp (mA) transformer
2.	15 kV 50 mA transformer
3.	spiral spark gap similar to "Jacob's Ladder"
4.	fluorescent tube with coil around upper part and rings around lower part
5.	stack of aluminum welding wire formed into individual spiral toroids on insulators
6.	small spark gap with spherical electrodes
7.	double-ended "dumbbell" Tesla coil
8.	small components not indicated on diagrams
9.	large variometer: a two-coil variable inductance device
10.	8" diameter air core coil
11.	main Tesla coil
12.	large aluminum sphere with adjustable-angle ring and coil wound around support, the "field shaper" or "ballast" to use John's terms

13. van de Graaff electrostatic machine of 200-300 kV DC
14. small components not indicated on diagrams
15. small components not indicated on diagrams
16. small components not indicated on diagrams
17. main “tuning” unit
18. 15 kV DC power supply
19. 15 kV DC capacitor with aluminum ring around electrode insulators
20. small components not indicated on diagrams
21. 30 kV DC insulation breakdown tester
22. small Tesla coil operating with two 811 power triode tubes
23. large loose-wound toroidal coil hung from ceiling
24. 10 kV 23 mA transformer
25. home-made “disruptive discharge” high voltage transformer after Tesla
26. 15 kV 30 mA transformer
27. 15 kV insulation breakdown tester
28. home-made assembly with quartz (?) crystal rods and toroidal coil
29. 15 kV 60 mA transformer
30. 21 kV 100 mA transformer
31. large flat spiral coil mounted on wall
32. large spark gap with spherical electrodes

The stack of toroids (5) is a curious device as can be seen from the photographs in Part III. For the electrical engineer, the toroids are only minimally capacitively coupled to one another, resulting in essentially zero power transfer (at 60 Hz) between any toroids on the stack. John used additional smaller toroid stacks as well, sometimes mounted horizontally on a wall. The fluorescent light unit (4) is just a fluorescent tube usually inserted in a copper tube with a loose coil wrapped around one end and one or two conductive rings close to the opposite end. Spherical spark gaps (6) and (32) generally never actually break down. Following the circuit diagram shows why.

The only conventionally-powered RF device is the small Tesla coil (22). The large Tesla coil (11) never receives real power input. Recall these are the actual detailed hookup diagrams, not block diagrams – nothing has been left out. Sometimes a connection was made to a toroid near the top ball of the large Tesla coil, which toroid was not electrically connected to the rest of the Tesla coil. On other occasions, a ring around the large Tesla coil's primary was part of the circuit, but was also not connected to the coil itself. It is obvious why the AC field strength readings I took showed such minuscule readings.

Item (28) was an assembly of a toroidal coil and several crystalline rods arranged around an axis with a pointed end looking like a futuristic "ray gun".

NC means that there is no electrical connection to that end of the device: it goes nowhere.

All the input power comes from the 110 VAC house mains supply via standard wall plugs. All the transformers shown are either directly connected to 110 V or via a voltage-controlling Variac. The other mains-powered devices are the van de Graaff's motor and the small Tesla coil. It is easy to see, therefore, why John used so little power for the apparatus.

As can be seen from Figures 1, 2 and 3, there are several components that are common to all circuits. Apparently, the essential arrangement consisted of the large Tesla coil (11), the dumbbell Tesla coil (7) and the field shaper (12). These components were usually arranged much as in the diagrams with the tip electrode of (7) an inch or two from the top ball of (11). A stiff wire hanging from the same tip of (7) came to within about 4 inches of (12). The van de Graaff machine (13) and uranium ore radioactive source (not shown in the circuit diagrams) completed the list of essential components.

The connection shown going to the base of the van de Graaff machine is an electrical connection to the lower brush assembly. Across gap (32) in Fig. 3 is one of John's aluminum foil Leyden jar –type capacitors.

The main points to be drawn from analysis of these circuits as well as observation of the photos in Part III are:

1. The configuration of the components changes each time the apparatus is set up.
2. The number and type of component parts change each time the apparatus is set up.
3. The vast majority of circuit connections are totally unintelligible to an electrical engineer.
4. The major components are not powered in the normal fashion.
5. The radio frequency field strengths are thus minuscule.
6. There is no apparent logic to the physical arrangement of the components.
7. The main "tuning" unit (17) plays no discernable role.
8. It is clear why the apparatus consumes so little mains power.

The inevitable conclusion from these observations is that the apparatus plays no primary role in producing the phenomena constituting the Hutchison Effect. Theories invoking aspects of the apparatus which have been put forward to explain the Hutchison Effect are essentially useless.[30]

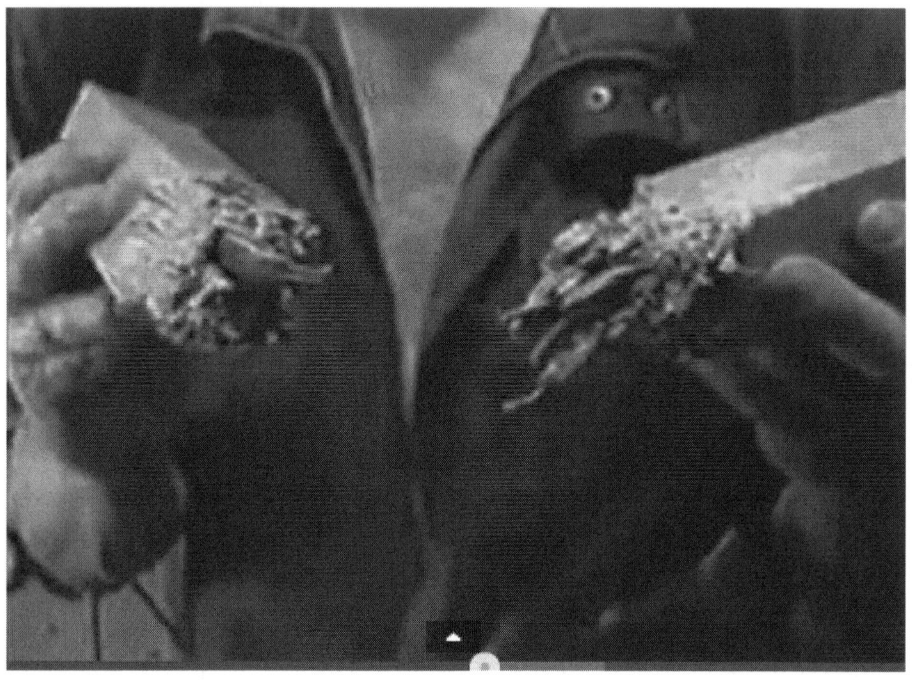

John holding two halves of an aluminum bar that was shredded in the center in what has subsequently been termed "disruption" that seemed to be focused along one plane or "active" region that sometimes was predictable. – Pub. Note

[30] Pub. Note: In defense of the synergistic benefits of John's circuit design, Dr. Andrija Puharich, who brought Uri Geller to the U.S. and to Targ and Puthoff's laboratory for testing (author of *Uri: A Journal of the mystery of Uri Geller* , 1974, on Amazon.com), also had a parapsychology lab of his own. His book *Beyond Telepathy* (Anchor Books, 1973, and still on Amazon.com) records improved telepathy results in narrative and table form of more than one subject when placed in a Faraday cage that is electrically "treated' and charged to high voltage of 10 to 20 kV DC. Dr. Puharich concludes, "It is believed that the environmental conditions of the Treated Faraday cage are essential for repeatable demonstration of telepathic interaction between two sensitives under acceptable scientific standards" (p. 224, Appendix A). It is left to the reader to decide if the argument for electrically enhanced telepathy extends to a case for electrically enhanced PK.

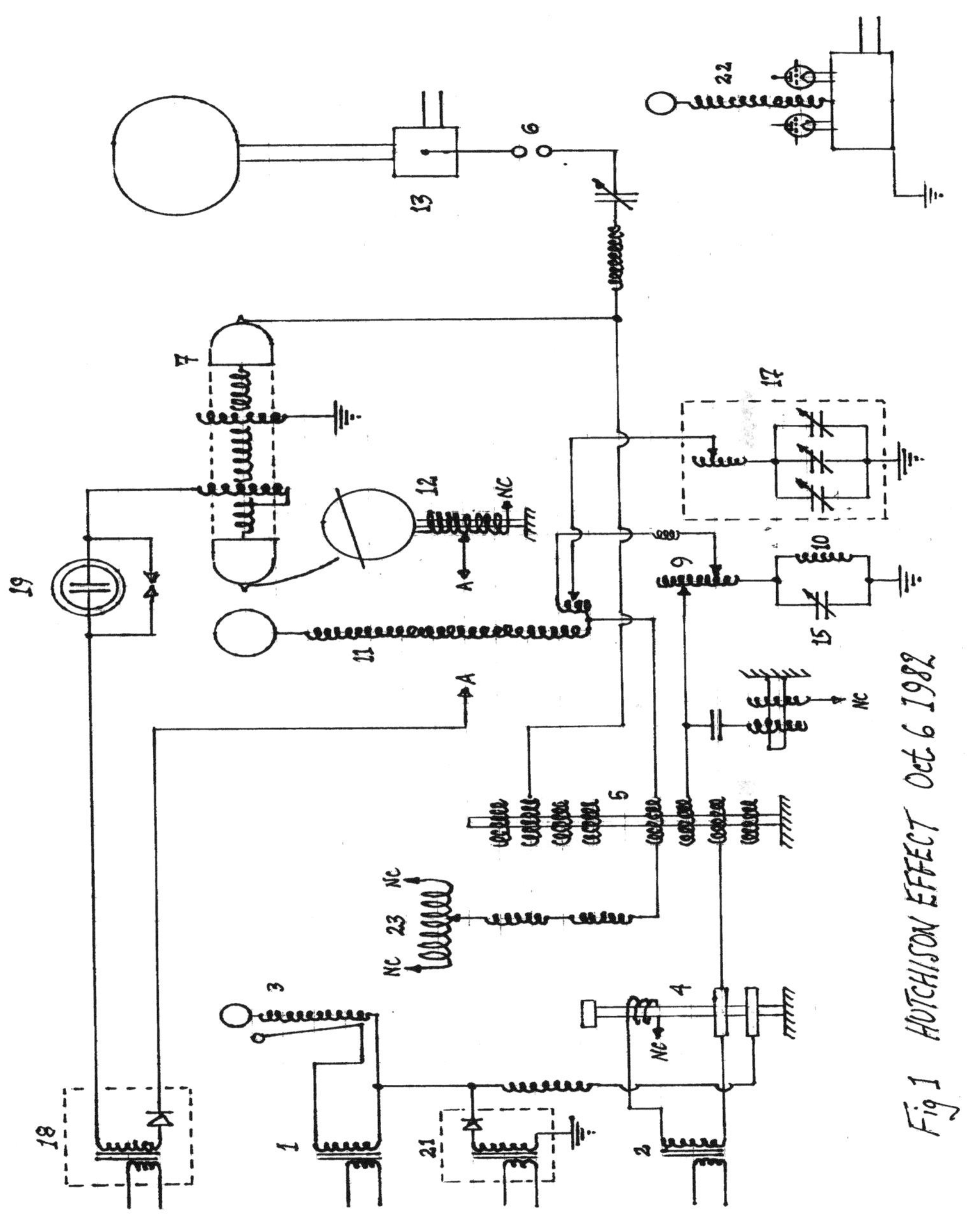

Fig 1 HUTCHISON EFFECT Oct 6 1982

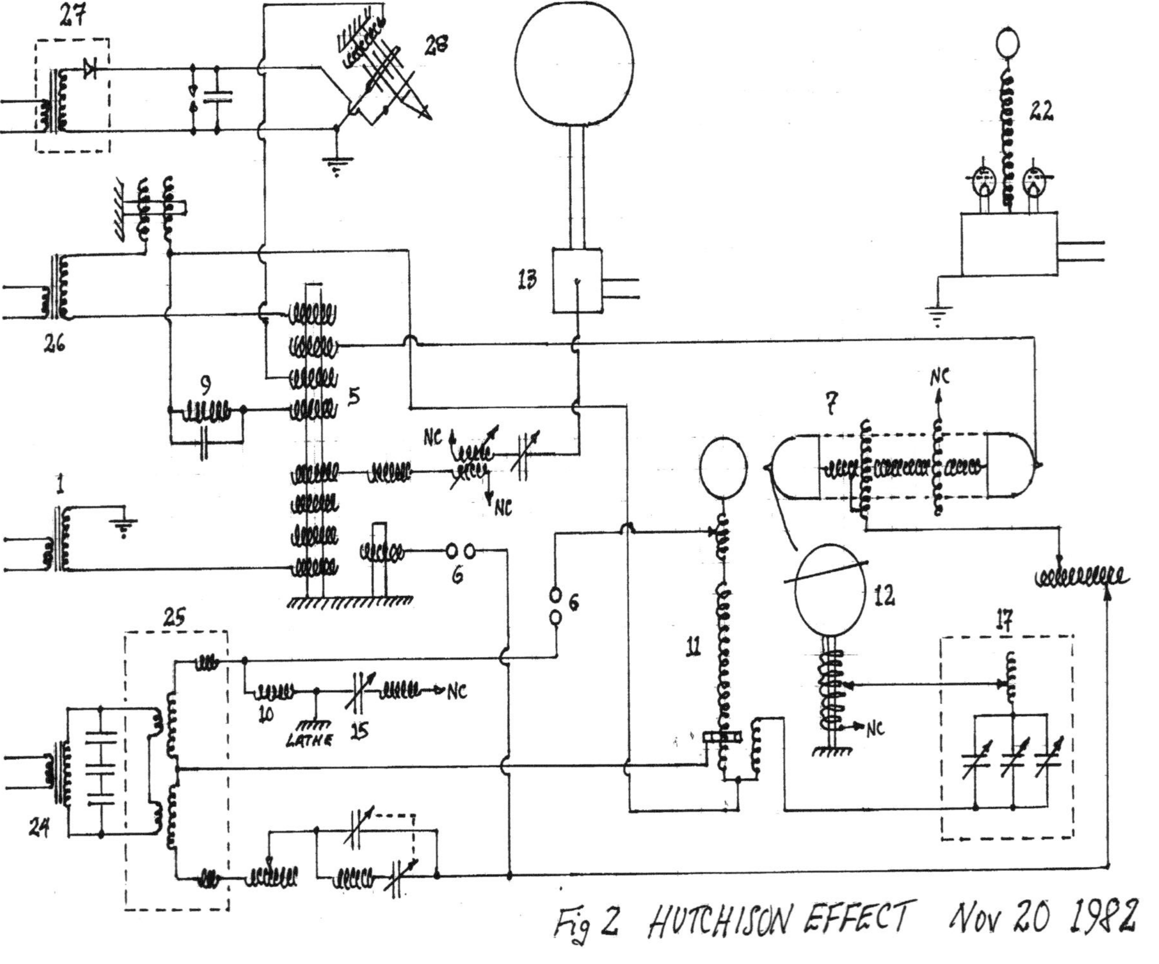

Fig 2 HUTCHISON EFFECT Nov 20 1982

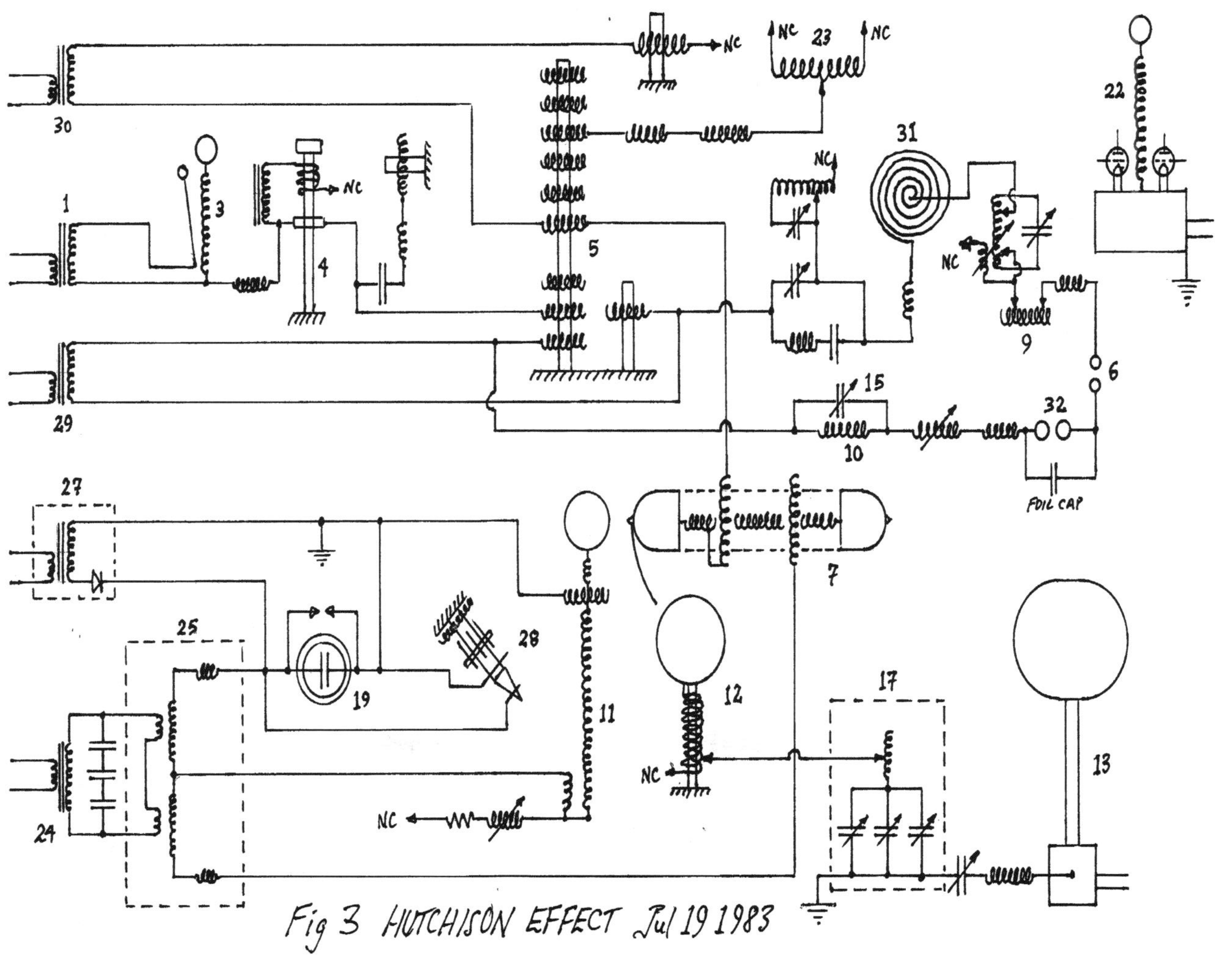

Fig 3 HUTCHISON EFFECT Jul 19 1983

Part III: Photo Gallery

The bulk of the following photographs are scanned reproductions of 35 mm colour slides taken at the time. They have been somewhat enhanced in brightness and contrast for this book.

Fig. 4. John Hutchison in 1982 outside his basement laboratory in the Murphy's home.

Fig. 5. The author and John outside the basement lab in the Murphy's home.

Fig. 6. Alex Pezarro and John outside the basement lab in the Murphy's home.

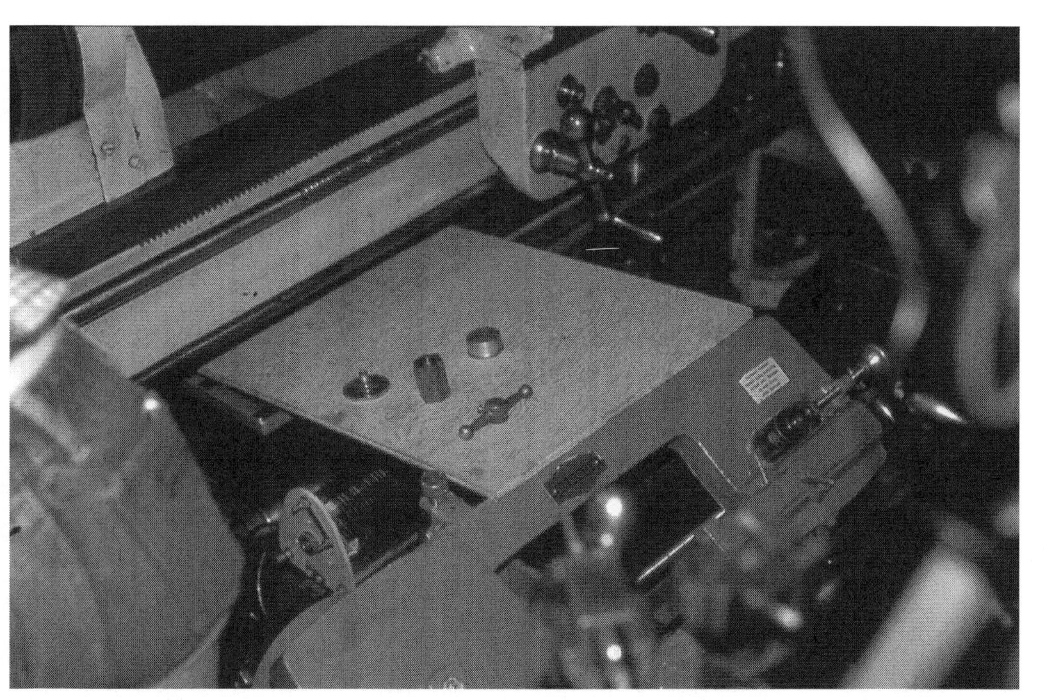

Fig. 7. Active area on plywood board between lathe and bandsaw.

Fig. 8. John with fractured steel bushing (on top of power supply cabinet) witnessed by this author and others.

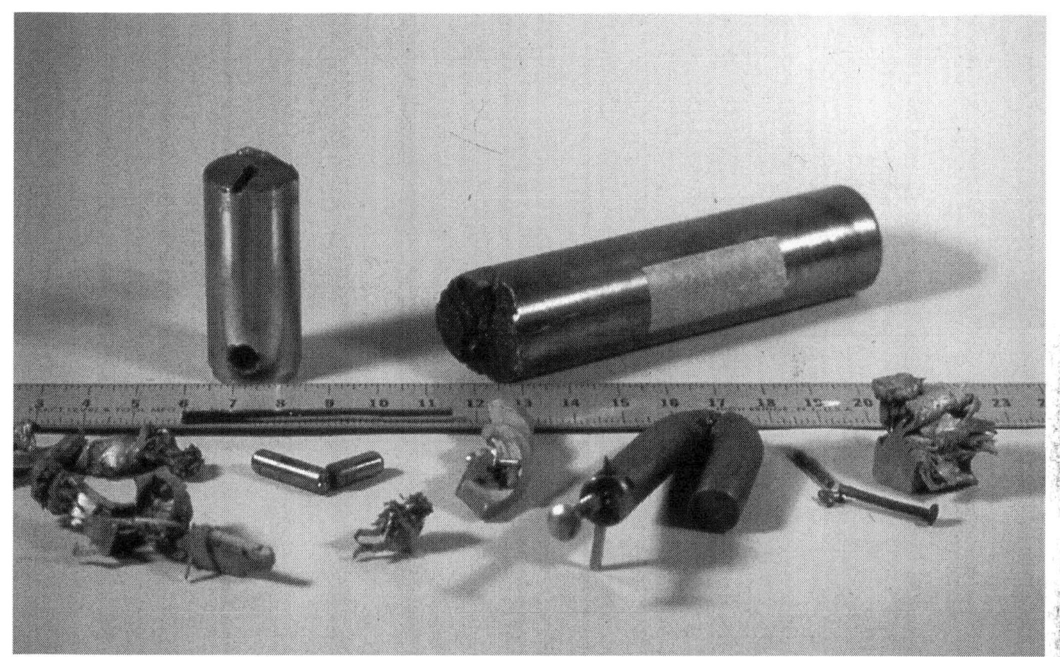

Fig. 9. Various fractured or bent metal samples (ruler scale in inches) from author's collection.

Foreground L to R: twisted aluminum bars, ALNICO cow magnet, small fractured aluminum bar, twisted aluminum angle bar, tightly bent and fractured steel boring bar, fractured and melted steel nail, de-laminated aluminum bar.

Behind ruler L to R: large case-hardened bar with case-hardening blown off at top, large steel bar with end part crumbled away.

On ruler: bent 5.5 inch long molybdenum rod supplied by Col. John Alexander

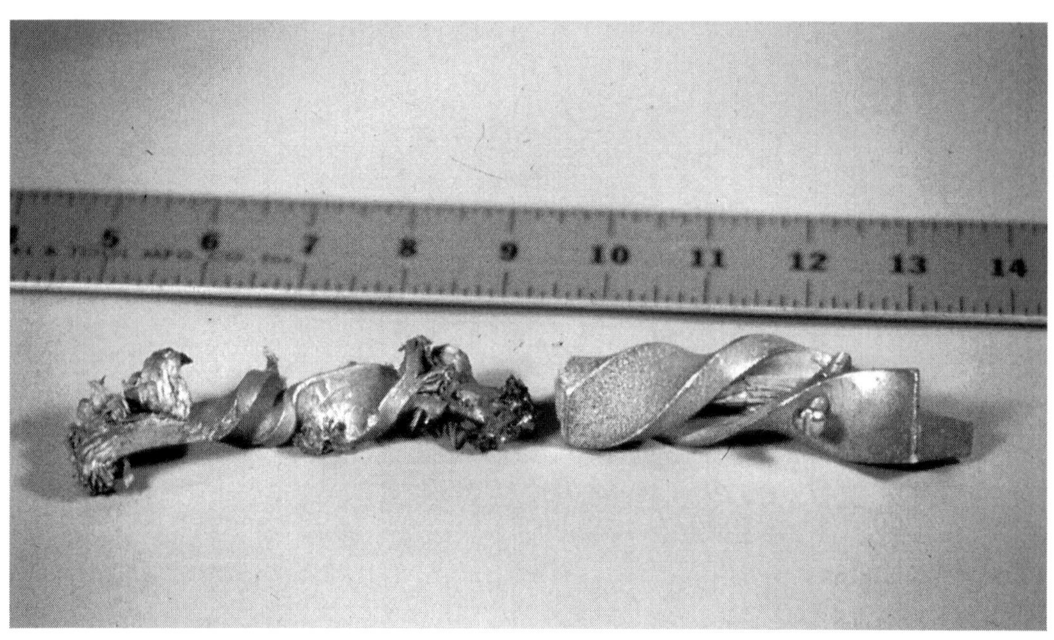

Fig 10. Close up of items in Fig. 9. Note captured piece of wood embedded in twisted aluminum angle bar showing no sign of heat.

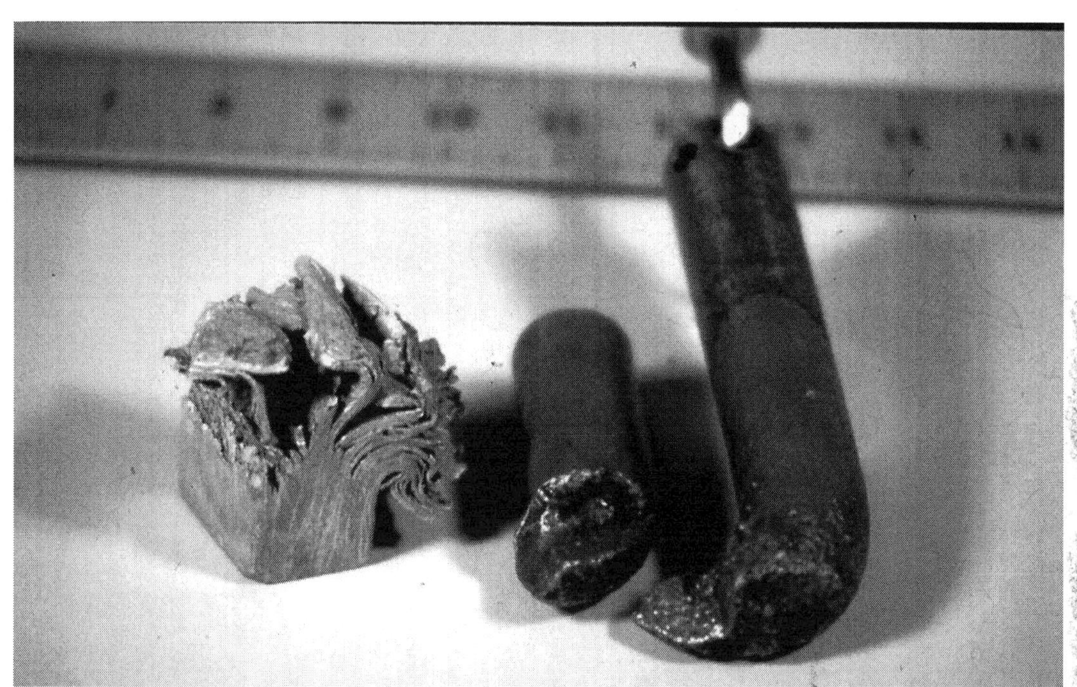

Fig. 11. Close up of items in Fig. 9. Colour photo shows small copper globules came out of solid solution at the fracture point of the steel boring bar.

Fig. 12. INSCOM demonstration.

L to R: Don Hendrix, Don Stefanik, Bob Freyman, Alex Pezarro, John Rink, John Alexander.

Fig. 13. Col. Alexander in foreground with John behind him, Alex Pezarro in doorway to INSCOM demonstration room. Note array of ping pong balls on mezzanine floor above demonstration room.

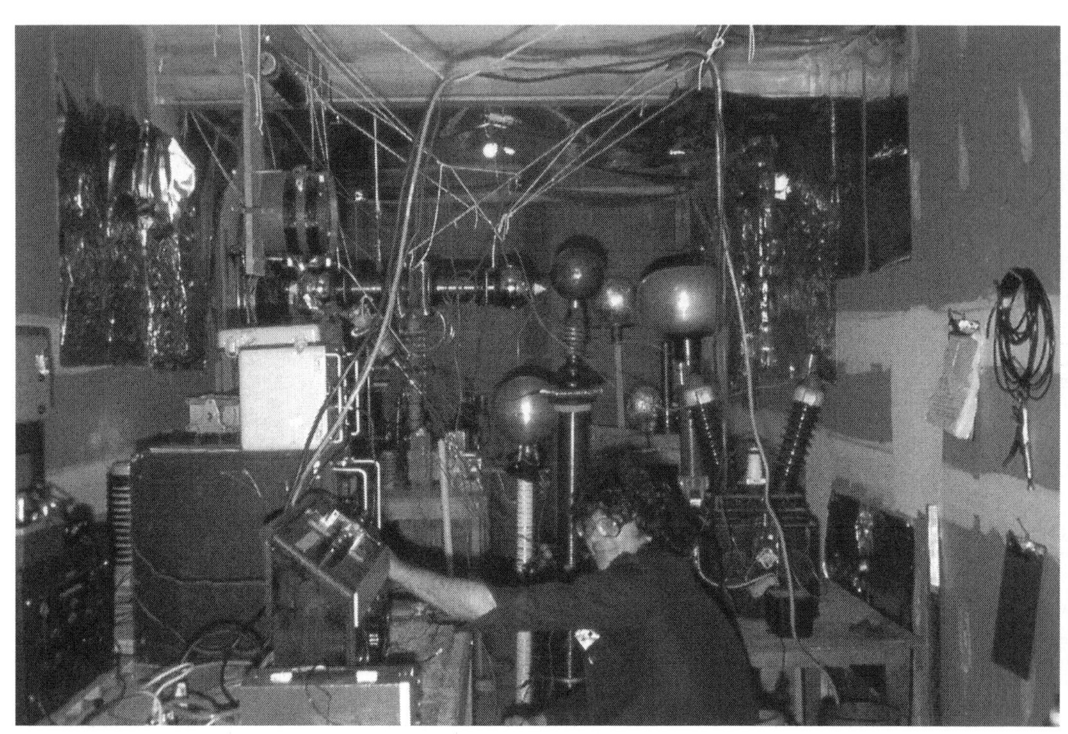

Fig, 14. John at the main tuning unit during the INSCOM demonstration. Main components are (L to R): large air core coil (above white box), dumbbell Tesla coil hanging from ceiling, “field shaper” large aluminum ball on white support tube, main Tesla coil, van de Graaff machine, disruptive discharge transformer (behind John and below van de Graaff).

Fig. 15. Small 2-tube Tesla coil on left with typical toroid stack on white insulators on right. Ping pong balls in background to check for effects outside the “active area”.

Fig. 16. John's "substation" power supply assembly with toroid stack on left, high voltage transformers at rear and right foreground, spiral spark gap rear right and fluorescent tube in copper pipe hanging from ceiling.

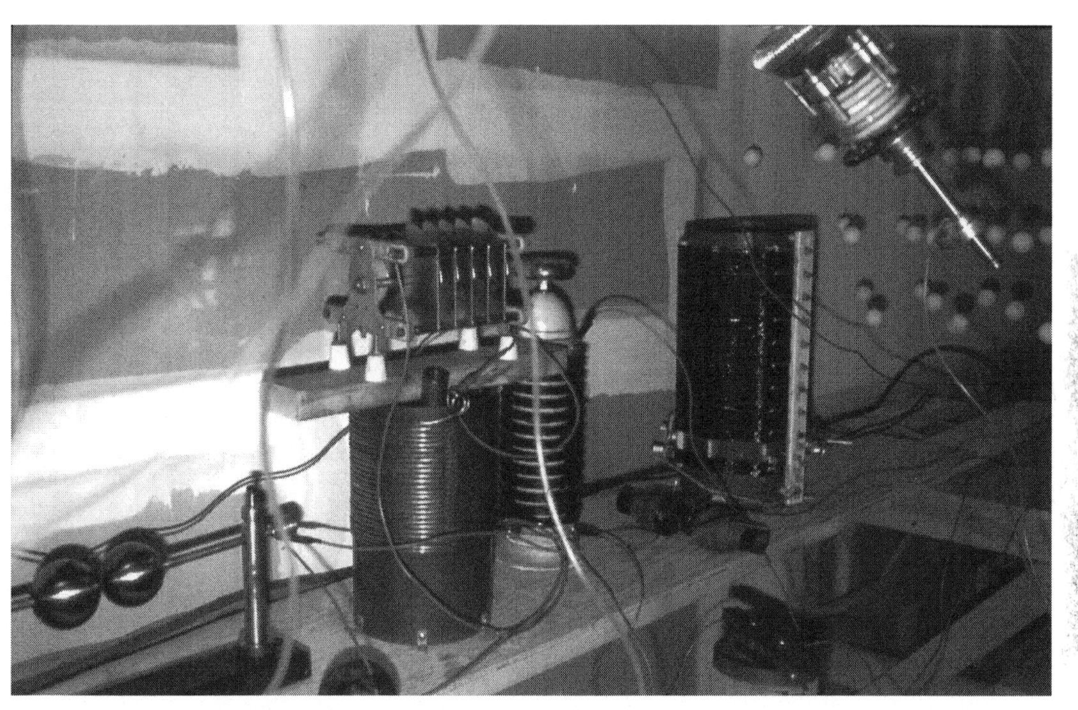

Fig. 17. From L to R: typical spherical electrode spark gap, tank coil/capacitor pair, RF choke, large multi-tapped variometer inductor, crystal unit hanging from ceiling.

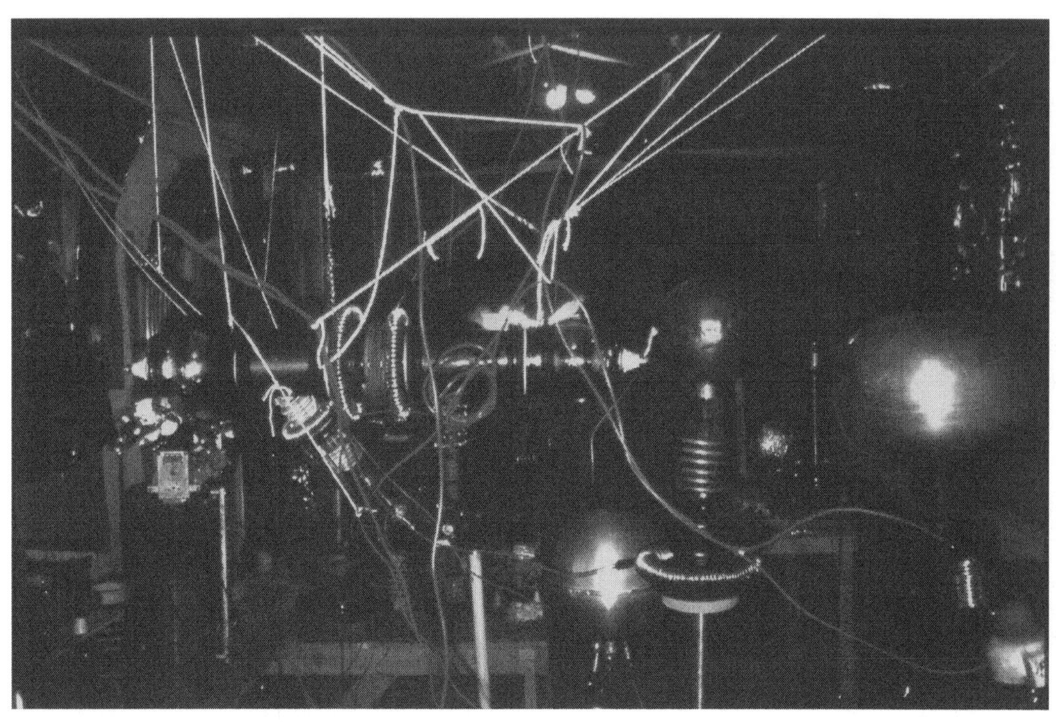

Fig. 18. Typical spontaneous fire on dumbbell Tesla coil (centre of picture) and RF arc between dumbbell coil and large Tesla coil ball.

Appendix[31]

It is worth noting that in 1994 a two-hour documentary video was produced by Lightworks AV called, "Free Energy: The Race to Zero Point" which subsequently sold thousands of copies and eventually was released to the internet by the producer: https://www.youtube.com/watch?v=aKWPht3fU-o . It is possible to fast forward to watch the 12-minute segment that features John Hutchison and several video clips of metal levitation and disruption, including the cannonball and a 19-pound bushing liftoff. In that segment, the technical consultant for the film, Tom Valone comments about the Hutchison Effect and displays a straight line graph based on some video stills of a 19-pound bushing lifting, supplied by George Hathaway. It is believed that the graph of the derivative of velocity vs. time (definition of acceleration), which normally results in a flat horizontal line showing a constant force or constant acceleration (e.g., using F=ma), is anomalous in this situation, since it is a straight slanted line which increases at a constant rate. This translates to a constantly increasing acceleration, which is relatively unknown on earth. Only the THIRD derivative results in a horizontal line or constant, which only can be called something else like "hyperacceleration" that is coined by Valone in the above documentary. One analogous situation exists in physics with the Abraham-Lorentz-Dirac equation that does exhibit a third derivative (rate of change of acceleration) called a "jerk" which is not constant however. Wikipedia is a good layman's reference source which explains the recoil force of emitted photon of electromagnetic radiation, also called "radiation reaction" which is proportional to the square of the object's charge times the jerk. The recoil force

[31] Pub. Note: This supplementary section has been added by the publisher to show the analytical possibilities of the Hutchison lift phenomenon, thanks to frame by frame images supplied by the author. Credit is due to George Hathaway for discovering and plotting the third derivative hyperforce of the Hutchison Effect, which was subsequently published in a PACE Newsletter by Valone.

points in the opposite direction as the velocity of the particle, such as an accelerating electron, providing a braking effect. Only an interdisciplinary physicist such as Puthoff or Tiller might be able to speculate on whether the Hutchison Effect manifestation of a third derivative hyperforce is related to the Abraham-Lorentz-Dirac equation.

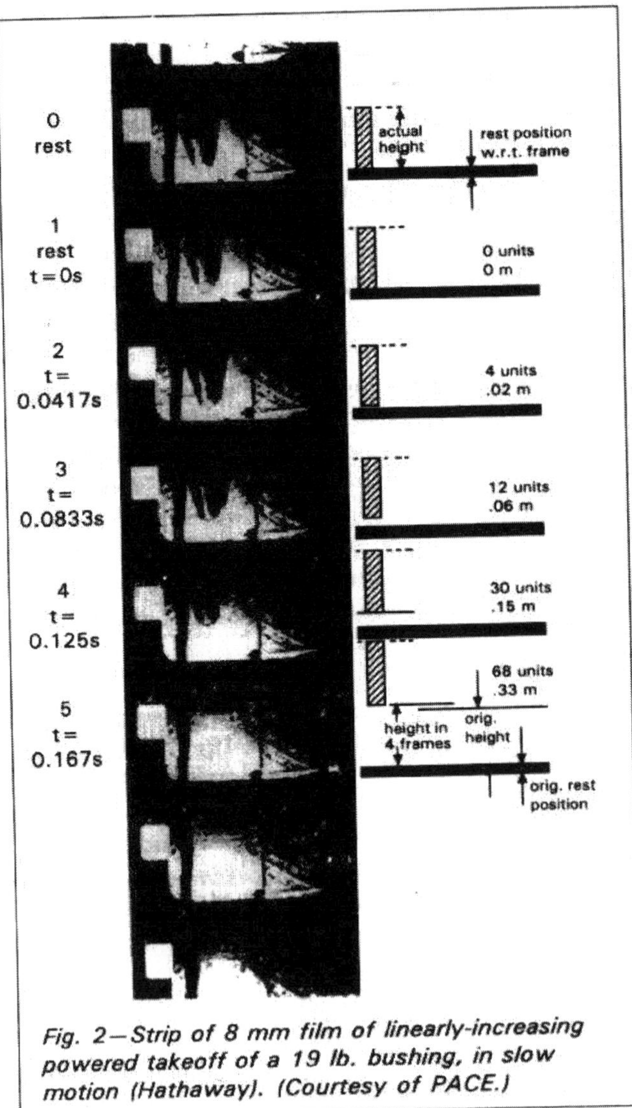

Fig. 2—Strip of 8 mm film of linearly-increasing powered takeoff of a 19 lb. bushing, in slow motion (Hathaway). (Courtesy of PACE.)

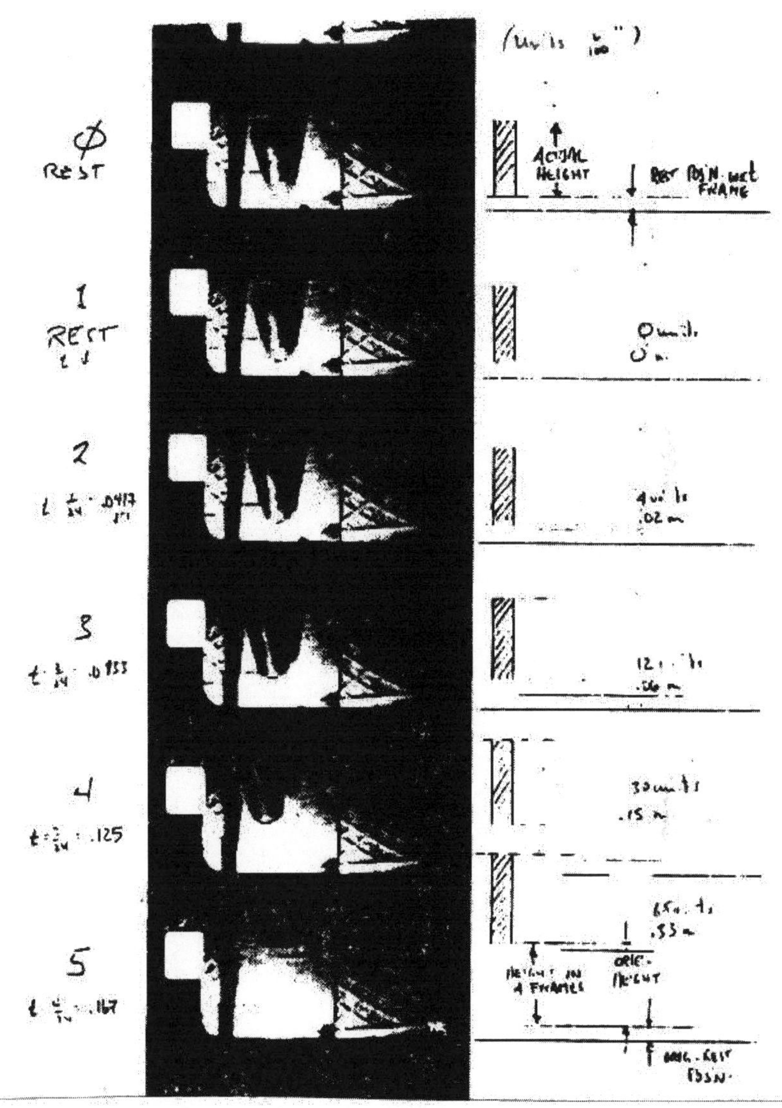

Original photo stills with hand-written notes by Hathaway

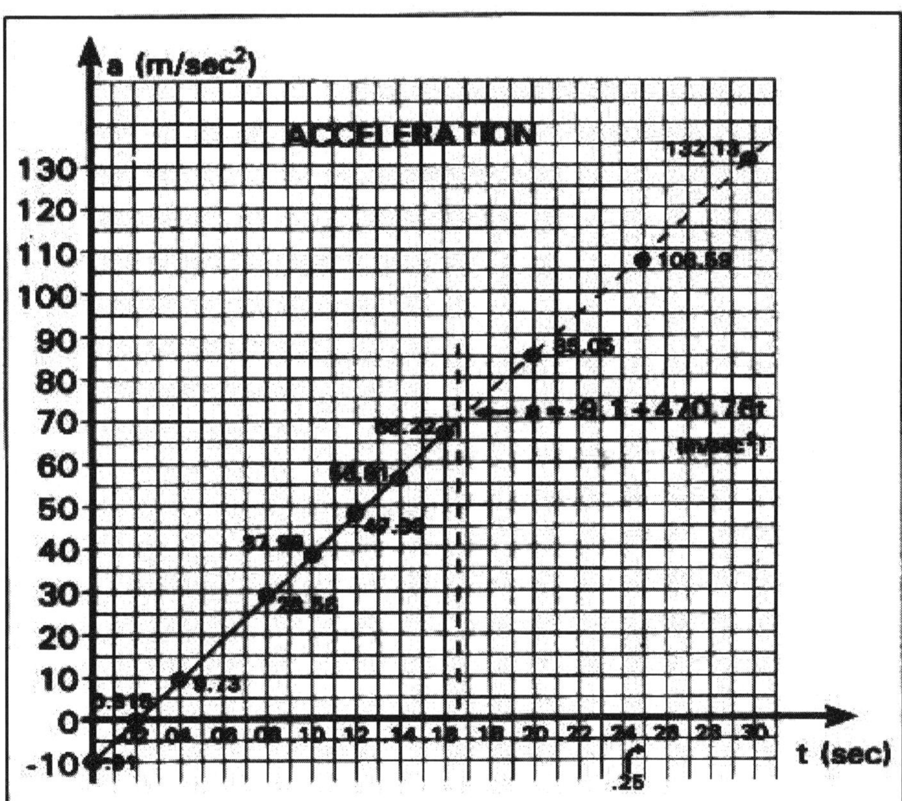

Fig. 3—Plot of linearly-rising powered take-off of a 19-lb. bushing calculated on an acceleration / time graph. Data plotted by George Hathaway.

DEPARTMENT OF THE ARMY

Vancouver, B.C.
Canada

Dear Mr. Hutchison:

Re: your letter December dated the 18 1990.

We understand that you received some slides of your work taked by Los Alamos and U.S.A.F 1983 June.

As you know the report is classified

Dear Mr. Hutchison:

Re: your letter December dated the 18 1990.

We understand that you received some slides of your work taked by Los Alamos and U.S.A.F 1983 June.

As you know the report is classified.

We suggest you go threw the proper foia act, The F.O.I.A. Title 5 Code 552.

However your project (The Hutchison Effect) holds merits in future developments

The best of luck in your research.

Previous page: 1991 letter to John Hutchison from the U.S. Department of the Army.

The body of the letter reads (with original spelling intact):

"Dear Mr. Hutchison,

Re: your letter December dated the 18 1990.

We understand that you received some slides of your work taken by Los Alamos and U.S.A.I 1983 June.

As you know the report is classified.

We suggest you go threw the proper foia act, The F.O.I.A. Title 5, Code 552.

However your project (The Hutchison Effect) holds merits in future developments.

The best of luck in your research."

INDEX

RELATED PUBLICATIONS from INTEGRITY RESEARCH INSTITUTE

ENGINEERING NON-CONVENTIONAL AC ELECTRICAL SYSTEMS by George Hathaway, PE, #119, 20 pages, $5

ELECTROGRAVITICS SYSTEMS, Vol. I, T. Valone, #611, 155 pages, $15
ELECTROGRAVITICS Vol. II, ed. by T. Valone, #615, 160 pages, $15

ZERO POINT ENERGY: THE FUEL OF THE FUTURE by Thomas Valone, #835, 246 pages, $22

THE INVENTION OF HANS COLER, by R. Hurst, #504, 34 pages, $6

ENERGETIC PROCESSES Vol. I, #413, 480 pages, $25
ENERGETIC PROCESSES Vol. ii, #415, 400 pages, $25

T.T. BROWN ELECTROGRAVITICS RESEARCH, edited by Thomas Valone, #603, 60 pages, $12

ELF MAGNETOMETER FOR EARTHQUAKE PREDICTION by Elizabeth Rauscher, PhD and T. Valone, #201, 28 pages, $6

THE ZINSSER EFFECT ed. by Thomas Valone, #701, 132 pages, $20

HARNESSING THE WHEELWORK OF NATURE: Tesla's Science of Energy by Thomas Valone, PhD, #117, 288 pages $ 16.95

BIOELECTROMAGNETIC HEALING: A Rationale for Its Use by Thomas Valone, PhD, *#414,* 132 Pages, $15.00

USE OF ELECTRICITY ON FACE AND SCALP, #419, 125 pages, $15

MINDBENDING: THE HUTCHISON FILES by George Hathaway, #719, 139 pages, $25

Note: *Add fixed $5 for Media mail or $7 for Priority mail no matter how many books by mail to IRI, 5020 Sunnyside Ave., Ste. 209, Beltsville MD 20705*
All major credit cards accepted. Please add expiration and three-digit code
Also, these are on Amazon.com and most are available for Kindle download
VISIT: IntegrityResearchInstitute.org or email for complete catalog

Call: 301-220-0440, Write or Email: iri@erols.com with address
Also see BioEnergyDevice.org and Futurenergy.org

R

S

T

V

W

Y

Z